'A treasure trove for every lover of Christmas carols -

unlikely stories of how our favourite carols came to be written, with insightful reflections on their deeper meaning.'

Sir John Rutter, composer and conductor

'What a glorious book – brimming with familiar carols, as well as overlooked treasures from down the years. We meet wonderful and talented characters who've created words or music, learn about the times they lived in, and hear engaging tales of their passion for singing to match their devotion to God. Filled with facts and faith, Gordon has provided us with an inspiring but practical reference book that surely is a "joy to the world"!'

Pam Rhodes, presenter on *Songs of Praise* and author

'Gordon Giles is, in my opinion, one of the pre-eminent hymn and carol experts of today. His insightful analyses, deft musical understanding and erudite theology all combine with a fantastic sense of humanity and compassion. This work is bursting with Gordon's characteristic integrity, warmth and wit. I heartily recommend it.'

Thomas Hewitt Jones, award-winning composer, music producer and songwriter

BRF Ministries

15 The Chambers, Vineyard
Abingdon OX14 3FE
+44 (0)1865 319700 | brf.org.uk

Bible Reading Fellowship (BRF) is a charity (233280)
and company limited by guarantee (301324),
registered in England and Wales

ISBN 978 1 80039 279 3
First published 2024
10 9 8 7 6 5 4 3 2 1 0
All rights reserved

Acknowledgements
Unless otherwise stated, scripture quotations are taken from the New Revised Standard
Version Updated Edition. Copyright © 2021 National Council of Churches of Christ in the
United States of America. Used by permission. All rights reserved worldwide. The quotations
marked NRSVA are taken from The New Revised Standard Version of the Bible, Anglicised
edition, copyright © 1989, 1995 by the Division of Christian Education of the National
Council of the Churches of Christ in the United States of America. Used by permission.
All rights reserved. The scripture quotation marked KJV is taken from The Authorised Version
of the Bible (The King James Bible), the rights in which are vested in the Crown, reproduced
by permission of the Crown's Patentee, Cambridge University Press.

The text of 'The Camel Carol' by Gordon Giles, © 2023 Stainer & Bell Ltd, 23 Gruneisen Road,
London N3 1LS, **www.stainer.co.uk**, is used by permission. All rights reserved.

A catalogue record for this book is available from the British Library

Printed and bound by Ashford Colour Press

A
CALENDAR
OF
CAROLS

GORDON GILES

Christmas reflections, prayers and songs of praise

Ministries

CONTENTS

ACKNOWLEDGEMENTS

Writing a book can be a lonesome journey, so it is always good to have companions on the way, with knowledge and a critical eye. This book is dedicated to the friends and family who helped, especially Stephen, Tommy and Stuart.

AUTHOR'S NOTE

Almost 20 years ago, in 2005, BRF Ministries published my book *O Come Emmanuel*, an Advent devotional book, which took the reader from 1 December to January 6, the feast of the Epiphany. Also published in an abbreviated form in the USA by Paraclete Press, that book similarly contains reflections upon carols and works of seasonal music. There is no overlap of content, even if one or two carols also find a place in this book. Readers who would like more might like to search out that older book.

INTRODUCTION

Come with me to 1843, the year Christmas was reinvented. The first Christmas cards were landing on doormats. As many as 2,050 Christmas cards had been sent using the Penny Post, introduced only three years earlier. They had cost a shilling each, and while nowadays the stamp can cost more than the card, in 1843 the card was by far the more expensive part of the equation. Sir Henry Cole, a well-known artist and designer of teapots, had been instrumental in the introduction of the Penny Post, and soon he had the brilliant and lucrative idea of introducing Christmas cards. His cards did not show the nativity or robins or Father Christmas, but rather a Dickensian family, drinking wine together and wishing each other 'A Merry Christmas and a happy new year to you.' In fact, only a few days after Cole began selling Christmas cards, Charles Dickens' *A Christmas Carol* was first published, on 19 December 1843. Christmas cards and Scrooge were both unleashed in the same week!

Christmas trees also began to take root, having been introduced by Prince Albert two years earlier in 1841. Meanwhile, 'God rest ye, merry gentlemen', 'The first Nowell',

'I saw three ships' and 'Hark the herald angels sing' were the latest hits, while 'Good King Wenceslas', 'It came upon the midnight clear' and 'O holy night' were soon to be written. It is fair to say that before 1840, there was Christmas, but not as we know it.

Very much in the spirit of the film *The Man Who Invented Christmas* (2017), which is all about how Charles Dickens came to write *A Christmas Carol* in 1843 and thereby changed attitudes to the 'festive season', his adopted home city of Rochester is swamped over the first weekend of Advent by festive activities. In the cathedral, carol services are presented at several times on the Saturday and Sunday. They are invariably packed with people who come to sing the Christmas favourites and hear the familiar story and a little sermon. As darkness falls past five o'clock, another carol service takes place on the stage in front of the castle, with a procession of costumed Dickens characters parading to sing the Christmas hits with a brass band, the Rochester Choral Society, the mayor of Medway and myself, as compere, and fake snow too!

It is a joyous sight and sound as the Christmas season gets underway. It sometimes clashes with Advent Sunday, which presents some logistical problems, as in the cathedral we are welcoming the season of darkness and light and preparing for the second coming, while outside the brass band are leading thousands of people in 'Silent night' at full volume. In 2023 the Advent carol service swiftly followed the communal Christmas carol-singing. Herein lies the Dickensian December double-think: Advent and Christmas must coexist for 25 days.

December is the month for Advent calendars, running from the first to the 24th day. If you are lucky, there will be a special window for Christmas Day too! Advent calendars, now so often filled with chocolates, teabags or even alcoholic miniatures, have become a celebratory daily indulgence. The Advent up-count, marked out by cardboard doorways, is actually a Christmas countdown, culminating with the virgin and child at the manger surrounded by shepherds and heralded by angels. (Strictly speaking any magi, kings or wise men should not appear in such an image, as they had not yet arrived! Artistic licence is often deployed, though.) This very book is something like it: each day we turn a page and open a doorway on to the life and meaning of a much-loved Christmas carol or hymn. Some are sweeter than others, and like chocolates in a more luxurious form of Advent calendar, we all have our favourites!

Thus in the double December world we inhabit, this month is both the countdown to Christmas and the upward-looking season of Advent. The two blend joyously, but if we look deeper into Advent there are bittersweet notes resonant of the Four Last Things (death, judgement, heaven and hell), and there are counterpoints which weave us back and forth into the world of Old Testament prophecy and prediction. We shall explore some of this as we travel through December, as through the doorways which open on to a carol, we see windows into scripture, and beyond, to salvation itself.

Gordon Giles

THE TIME OF GRACE

Gaudete!

*Gaudete! Gaudete!
Christus est natus
ex Maria virgine,
Gaudete!*

*Tempus adest gratiæ
hoc quod optabamus
carmina letitiæ
devote reddamus.*

*Now rejoice! Now rejoice!
Jesus the Christ is born
of the virgin Mary,
so rejoice!*

As the time of grace now brings
hope for all creation,
let us now our praises sing,
dancing with devotion.

Deus homo factus est
natura mirante
mundus renovatus est
a Christo regnante.

Human flesh our God takes on,
nature stands in wonder,
Christ our king, salvation won,
casts all doubts asunder.

Ezechielis porta
clausa pertransitur
unde lux est orta
salus inuenitur.

Passing through Ezekiel's gate,
opened for redemption,
brings our world a better fate,
hope for every nation.

Ergo nostra concio
psalatjam in lustro
benedicat Domino
salus regi nostro.

Therefore let God's people sing
songs of restoration;
let us bless the Lord our king,
bringer of salvation.

Words and Music: Piae Cantiones, compiled 1582 by Theodoric Petri of Nyland (c. 1560–1630), ed. Jacobus Petri Finno (c. 1540–88), Jaakko Suomalainen ('Finno'); translated by Gordon Giles (b. 1966)

We begin our December journey with a song which typifies and sets the tone for the Advent season. Derived from the Latin word for 'rejoice', 'Gaudete!' invites us to embrace the joy that comes with the anticipation of Christ's birth. For many, this is what Advent is about: preparation to celebrate the first coming of the Messiah, the incarnation. The four Sundays of Advent count us down to Christmas as a sort of weekly Advent calendar. The third Sunday of Advent is actually called Gaudete Sunday in some traditions.

The refrain of this 16th-century song is a call to *gaudete* – to rejoice. While it has a simple message, it is hard to translate into English in singable form because of its irregular rhythm. It draws on Philippians 4:4–5: 'Rejoice in the Lord always; again I will say, Rejoice. Let your gentleness be known to everyone. The Lord is near.' The nearness of the Lord, whose second coming might be a cause of caution, is here presented by Paul as a reason for rejoicing. The music and words make that clear: it is a joyous Advent leading to a greater joy of Christmas incarnation to which this song directs us. Sometimes thought of as an Advent song, or carol, or even as a Christmas carol, that it is a call to rejoice, to worship, makes it more akin to a hymn. Those who sing it do so on behalf of those who listen, for the text invites, if not commands, us all to join in the song of rejoicing.

This is true whether we are in church, listening to a concert or tuning into Steeleye Span's rendition from 1972, which made it into the charts on their fourth album *Below the Salt*. The record sleeve notes described it thus:

Mist takes the morning path to wreath the willows – Rejoice, rejoice – small birds sing as the early rising monk takes to his sandals – Christ is born of the Virgin Mary – cloistered, the Benedictine dawn threads timelessly the needles eye – rejoice.

They issued a different version as a single with 'The holly and the ivy' as a B-side. Re-released in November 1973, it reached no. 14 and was their first chart success. They used it again as a B-side to 'The boar's head carol' in 1977. It is one of only two top 20 UK hits to be sung entirely in Latin! (The other was 'Pie Jesu' from Andrew Lloyd Webber's *Requiem*).

The original work is somewhat veiled in those Benedictine mists. No music was provided in the Finnish songbook in which it first appeared, *Piae Cantiones* ('Pious songs'), which was published by a character some refer to as Finno (the Finnish man), who probably wrote the refrain. It was sung to the tune of a Czech Christmas song. The words can be traced to a medieval Bohemian song called 'Ezechielis porta' ('Ezekiel's gate'), which Finnish students of theology might have picked up in Prague.

There is also a connection to the German reformer Martin Luther, whose mealtime grace 'Danket dem Herrn' ('Thank the Lord') was sung to a tune which, according to *The New Oxford Book of Carols*, may have been adapted for this song. I can find no evidence for this. However, Luther would surely have approved of the first verse, which resonates with Paul's saying: 'For by grace you have been saved through faith, and this is not your own doing; it is the gift of God' (Ephesians 2:8). The same 'grace' is found in the second verse, which speaks of the incarnation, of God made man: 'And the Word became flesh and lived among us, and we have seen his glory, the glory as of a father's only son, full of grace and truth' (John 1:14).

The third verse brings in an Old Testament reference to Ezekiel's vision of the eastern gate of the city:

> Then he brought me back to the outer gate of the sanctuary that faces east, and it was shut. The Lord said to me: 'This gate shall remain shut; it shall not be opened, and no one shall enter by it, for the Lord, the God of Israel, has entered by it; therefore it shall remain shut. Only the prince, because he is a prince, may sit in it to eat food before the Lord; he shall enter by way of the vestibule of the gate and shall go out by the same way.'
> EZEKIEL 44:1–4

The meaning in the lyrics is that Jesus is the prince, the son of the Lord God of Israel, who via the womb of the virgin Mary enters and redeems the world in a way no one else can. Ezekiel's gate is closed to all except the Saviour. Simultaneously the gate can be seen as a symbol of Mary's perpetual virginity.

The fourth verse, which does not appear in some versions, reiterates the acclamation of celebration in response to salvation brought by the king of salvation, Christ, born of the virgin Mary, in whom we rejoice.

We rejoice in the promise of a return of Christ at the culmination of all things which we call the second coming; we rejoice in the festivities of December heralding the dawn of Christmas morn. We hold these two in delightful tension and relish the beautiful dance music which both accompanies and illustrates our festive journey.

God, as we begin the journey of Advent on the busy road to Christmas, help us sing your praises with joyful hearts and voices, that we may hear the rhythms of redemption and the harmonies of hope revealed in our Lord and King, Jesus Christ. Amen.

2 OF ONE THAT IS SO FAIR AND BRIGHT

Hymn to the virgin

O f one that is so fair and bright,
    velut maris stella, [like a star of the sea]
Brighter than the day is light,
    parens et puella. [mother and maiden]
I cry to thee, thou see to me
    Lady, pray thy Son for me, *Tampia* [thou Holy One]
That I may come to thee. *Maria!* [Mary]

All this world was forlorn
    Eva peccatrice [through Eve, the sinner]
Till our Lord was yborn
    de te genetrice [of thee, the mother]
With *ave* it went away [hail]
    darkest night, and comes the day *salutis* [of salvation]
The well springeth out of thee *virtutis.* [of virtue]

Lady, flower of everything,
    rosa sine spina, [rose without a thorn]
Thou bare Jesu, heaven's king
    gratia divina: [by divine grace]
Of all that bear'st the prize
    Lady, queen of paradise, *Electa.* [chosen one]
Maid mild, mother *es effecta*. [thou art proved]

Words: anonymous, circa 1300
Music: Benjamin Britten (1913–76)

Benjamin Britten's 'Hymn to the virgin' is not the easiest one in the Christmas choral repertoire, but it has something very important to show us as we prepare for carol services, concerts and street-singing in the upcoming 'festive season', as many call it.

When he wrote it, in 1930, he was 17. It is a macaronic carol; that is, it mixes lyrics in Latin and English. The choir sing in two languages, alternately: one is ancient and barely comprehensible; the other a bit old-fashioned, but recognisable.

In performance the choir is split with a few voices often separated spatially too, perhaps in a gallery or at the back of a church. Thus the audience or congregation may find themselves in between the two choirs, and this can create an ethereal effect. One choir sings in Old English and the other in Latin, and they respond to each other musically and linguistically. It is thought that the tradition of macaronic carols goes back to a time when medieval clergy wanted to retain a liturgical, spiritual dimension in the midst of popular vernacular songs. Writers therefore blended the sacred and secular languages, to avoid falling foul of church leaders, yet to appeal to popular culture.

The text is sung to Mary, mother of Jesus, and opens with the medieval Catholic understandings of her identity as the 'star of the sea' (*stella maris*), guiding sailors. The Roman Catholic mission to those at sea is still called Stella Maris to this day. As the mother of Jesus, Mary has a special place among the saints, through whom prayers and intercessions may be made for others, for safety and guidance. Note that the prayers are not directed to her, but request that she may 'pray for me'. The idea is that because she is close to Jesus, in heaven as on earth, perhaps closer than any other saint, she can pray for those on earth who make such requests.

The second verse concludes by stating that the wellspring of salvation – Jesus – sprang from her womb. This gives Mary unique significance and power. Because she bore Jesus, she is to be prized and praised above all as the 'queen of heaven'. Such is the medieval thinking which is still retained in Roman Catholic and other devotion to Mary.

In this choral carol we find 20th-century musical style blended with medieval Latin and English texts which present a worldview and ecclesiology that is alien to so many today. Yet one does not have to be a medieval, or even 21st-century, Catholic to appreciate the spatial impact and beauty of the melody and harmony, which not only add to the words, but may even render them secondary. The words are opaque, but the gentle, devotional feel touches hearts and minds.

For many this is necessary and sufficient. While surveys may indicate that around half the UK population consider Jesus to be irrelevant to Christmas, or deny believing the main aspects of the nativity story, many people attend Christmas services in church. Others say that Christmas is 'for the children'. Many who attend Christmas services are not regular churchgoers and they say that they go 'because of the music'. They like the carol service to be candlelit, and the carols to be 'traditional'. Parish and cathedral clergy and musical directors know full well that Christmas carol services do not provide a great deal of scope for creative programming. There are hymns and carols which cannot be omitted without causing disappointment.

Churches that offer Nine Lessons and Carols by candlelight on the Sunday before Christmas are providing exactly what the people want, it seems. Christmas is the busiest and most 'successful' time of the year for clergy and musicians. For many the period between lunchtime on Christmas Eve and Christmas Day is a long haul, at least rewarded by appreciative congregations, many of whom come at no other time of year. Most musicians and clergy do enjoy Christmas, even as they wrestle with the two-fold challenge of it all: the physical, mental challenge of delivering high-quality, gospel-focused coherent and intellectually satisfying Christmas services and sermons; and the challenge to cut through the tinsel to truly wonder whether the wonder of Christmas has touched souls as well as stomachs. Those who lead Christmas services want the angels' song of '*Gloria in excelsis Deo*' to be not only heard, but also taken into the hearts of hearers, who, even if they do not begin to attend weekly, will go away perhaps changed for the better.

In Britain at least, during Advent and at Christmas itself, we have to do what the young Benjamin Britten's 'Hymn to the virgin' embodies perfectly: we need to sing in two languages. While many people lament the secularisation of Christmas (and always have done, incidentally), the direction that Christmas takes nowadays needs to be put into historical context – related to the relatively recent popularity of Christmas carols and ultimately seen as an opportunity not a problem. Carols are not simply nice tunes with empty words to those who sing and preach, but are what we truly believe and act upon as, year by year, we present the good news of the birth of Christ in every and any language.

God and Father of our Lord Jesus Christ, as we hear, once again, the message of the angels, let it be our care and delight as we read and mark in scripture your loving purposes revealed in the incarnation of your Son, the same Christ our Lord. Amen.

3 A COLD AND FROSTY MORNING

Past three a clock

*Past three a clock,
    and a cold frosty morning.
Past three a clock,
good morrow, masters all!*

Born is a baby,
gentle as may be,
Son of the eternal
Father supernal.

Seraph quire singeth,
angel bell ringeth;
hark how they rime it,
time it and chime it.

Mid earth rejoices
hearing such voices;
e'ertofore so well
carolling Nowell.

Hinds o'er the pearly
dewy lawn early
seek the high stranger
laid in the manger.

Cheese from the dairy
bring they for Mary,
and, not for money,
butter and honey.

Light out of star-land
leadeth from far land
princes, to meet him,
worship and greet him.

Myrrh from full coffer,
incense they offer;
nor is the golden
nugget withholden.

Thus they: I pray you,
up, sirs, nor stay you
till ye confess him
likewise and bless him.

Words: George Ratcliffe Woodward (1848–1934)
Music: 'London waits', from W. Chappell's *Popular Music of the Olden Time*, arranged by Charles Wood (1866–1926)

One of the most significant, but now almost unknown, Christmas carol collections of the last hundred years or so is *The Cambridge Carol Book*. Sadly, much of its content is unusable today, as much of it was a century ago. Its words editor, George Ratcliffe Woodward, had a penchant for archaisms, and the volumes he edited often included ancient or quasi-ancient texts he penned himself.

Born in Birkenhead, Woodward was educated in Elstree, Hertfordshire, then at Harrow School. In 1867 he went to Gonville and Caius College, Cambridge, graduating in 1872. During that time, he encountered Anglo-Catholicism and experienced plain-song, which remained a lifelong interest. He also played the cello and the euphonium, and enjoyed beekeeping and, significantly, bell-ringing, a pastime which he drew upon to write 'Ding dong, merrily on high!'

In 1892 Woodward published a collection of twelve carols called *Carols for Christmas-Tide*, which brought him into contact with the Irish composer Charles Wood. This led to a friendship and collaboration until Wood's death in 1926. In 1893 came a sequel, *Carols for Christmas-Tide, Series II*, containing nine items. Then *Carols for Easter and Ascension-tide* contained twelve items, including an original composition, 'This joyful Eastertide'.

In 1924 Woodward and Wood published *The Cambridge Carol Book: Being fifty-two songs for Christmas, Easter and other seasons*. Woodward 'edited' the volume with Wood, but much of its content was original, and it included 'Ding dong, merrily on high!' and 'Past three a clock', which is also still popular. The refrain of the latter is old, but the rest of the carol was newly composed by Woodward, and the tune, 'London waits', from W. Chappell's *Popular Music of the Olden Time*, was harmonised by Wood. The words of the refrain had appeared in John Playford's *Dancing Master* (1665) and were often quoted in the 18th and 19th centuries.

One of the tasks of the groups of musicians known from medieval times as the 'waits' was to call out the time (the hours) during the night, and this carol is probably derived from a call of the London City waits, greeting the dawn – although 3.00 am does seem far too early to get up! The juxtaposition of the waits' early morning cry with verses about the Christmas story is novel, but it creates a vision of quasi-medieval – or perhaps Dickensian – hustle and bustle as a new Christmas morning dawns in an imaginary London. Woodward's characteristic use of archaisms makes the carol appear more authentic than it is. Some of the verses are distinctly odd for sure: the idea of bringing milk from the dairy for Mary and honey for no money is contrived, even if one might connect a reference to the promised land 'flowing with milk and honey' (Exodus 3:8).

The carol reveals what Woodward was trying to do in almost all his work: blend a quaint, domesticated understanding of Christmas goodwill with the nativity story, making it not just homely, but bringing it into the home, so that it should be taken into the hearth and heart, inspiring those who sing to 'own' the story and the deeper meaning it conveys. There are many reasons why so much of his material has now sunk without trace, but the strength of the jaunty tune of 'Past three a clock' has given it an enduring place in the Christmas repertoire. Arguably it is neither better nor worse than many of Woodward's other carols, but it has captured the imagination of publishers and singers alike.

The Cambridge Carol Book was not a success, and its weaknesses prompted the creation of *The Oxford Book of Carols* in 1928. That book, which was bigger, better and more scholarly, moulded a tradition which in 1961 saw the advent of *Carols for Choirs*, a series published by Oxford University Press, which now has six volumes and forms the backbone of the English-singing Christmas choral tradition. 'Past three a clock', 'Ding dong, merrily on high!' and 'The Linden Tree Carol' are the only three items that travelled from Cambridge to Oxford, and which consequently are with us still.

What Woodward tried and frequently failed to do can be seen as an attempt to achieve what some have more readily done a century later, which is to surreptitiously mix the gospel account with popular culture. In December the shops blare out hymns which sing of 'joy to the world', harking to herald angels and acknowledging that 'Christ the Saviour is born' on what is a most 'holy night'. These phrases and the hymns in which they are found are heard intermingled with 'White Christmas' (the world's biggest-selling single, in physical copies, at over 50 million), 'The Little Drummer Boy' and 'All I Want for Christmas Is You'.

We saw yesterday with 'Hymn to the virgin' how at Christmas we need to sing metaphorically in two languages at once. This carol, which combines not two languages but two styles – the ancient and the modern – likewise reminds us of that need. The history of carol singing is a story of how writers and composers have combined ancient and medieval traditions (or at least their understandings of them) with modern appeal. Or, to put it simply, Christmas carols are all about telling and interpreting an old story in a new way. Woodward used his somewhat quaint and unique ability to write quasi-medieval carols to do exactly that.

O God, you are master of us all at all times of day and night. Grant as we sing your praises as best we may, that we may be reminded not only of the Christmas story, but of the greater narrative of human sin and salvation of which it speaks. May we worship and greet Jesus, and confess and bless your holy name. Amen.

GLORIA, IN EXCELSIS!

Ding dong, merrily on high!

Ding dong, merrily on high!
In heaven the bells are
ringing;
ding dong, verily the sky
is riv'n with angels singing.
Gloria, hosanna in excelsis!

E'en so here below, below,
let steeple bells be swungen,
and *io*, *io*, *io*,
by priest and people sungen.
Gloria, hosanna in excelsis!

Pray you, dutifully prime
your matin chime, ye ringers;
may you beautifully rime
your evetime song, ye singers.
Gloria, hosanna in excelsis!

Words: George Ratcliffe Woodward (1848–1934)
Music: 'Branle de l'Official' in *Orchésographie*,
Jehan Tabourot (1520–95)

This carol was written by the same serious-minded Anglican clergyman who wrote 'Past three a clock' (see yesterday's reflection) and whose influence upon and contribution to the musical aspects of a modern Christmas are immeasurable. Published in 1924 by SPCK, with Woodward as words editor and Charles Wood (1866–1926) as musical editor, *The Cambridge Carol Book* introduced us to 'Ding dong, merrily on high!' as well as 'Past three a clock'. Undoubtedly the most famous of Woodward's carols, he wrote words for a tune from the *Orchésographie* of 1588 by Thoinot Arbeau (1520–95), whose real name was Jehan Tabourot.

Tabourot was a priest who enjoyed dancing, and his *Orchésographie* was the only dance manual published in France in the second half of the 16th century. It provides invaluable and unique information about the nature, style and performance practices of his age, although in it he provided only melodies, expecting harmonies to be improvised. Wood harmonised the 'Branle de l'Official', with its extended setting of the 'Gloria' and use of the expression of joy, '*io*', which combine with the macaronic use of English and Latin to create a rather exotic mix:

And io, io, io
by priest and people sungen
Gloria, hosanna in excelsis!

The style of 'Ding dong, merrily on high!' is characteristic of Woodward's delight in archaic poetry. This, combined with the 16th-century tune which Wood then harmonised, means that, though the song is barely a century old, it appears to be an ancient carol. Nevertheless it has became a firm favourite in church, shop and street. Its mix of linguistic idiom serves as a metaphor for the modern trend, need even, to blend the three aspects of gospel, tradition and contemporary relevance in a single song.

In this is the modern phenomenon of Christmas most clearly demonstrated. As a Christmas carol it takes its reference point and refrain from scripture: the angels' song to the shepherds. Yet it is obscure and uses a foreign language from long ago, far away. It blends the somewhat romantic, but nevertheless real, concept of church bells rung by a band of local people – the near and the distant, the exotic and the immediate are combined. With made-up exclamations, a sense of mystery is also added, meaningless as 'io, io, io' may be.

Yet the true meaning is in the message, and the bell-ringers are, in fact, the angels bringing – and ringing – the good news of the incarnation. Bells summon the people to church – that is their official purpose – and that is what the angels did for the shepherds when they proclaimed, 'Gloria in excelsis':

The angel said to them, 'Do not be afraid, for see, I am bringing you good news of great joy for all the people: to you is born this day in the city of David a Saviour, who is the Messiah, the Lord. This will be a sign for you: you will find a child wrapped in bands of cloth and lying in a manger.' And suddenly there was with the angel a multitude of the heavenly host, praising God and saying,

'Glory to God in the highest heaven,

and on earth peace among those whom he favours!'

When the angels had left them and gone into heaven, the shepherds said to one another, 'Let us go now to Bethlehem and see this thing that has taken place, which the Lord has made known to us.' So they went with haste and found Mary and Joseph and the child lying in the manger. When they saw this, they made known what had been told them about this child.

LUKE 2:10–17

Faith transcends language and is nourished by a call – a summons – to drop everything and go to worship the one who is the newborn king and Saviour of the world. The shepherds did it, and it is what our bellringers of today bid us do, not only at Christmas but every time they ring. They call us to prayer, they proclaim Christ as captain of the church and tower and they make the noise of joyful praise.

Ringing bells tell us something has happened or is about to happen. In times of sorrow or strife they warn or remind us of sadness, such as when Queen Elizabeth II died. They ring the knell of sombre sorrow, muffled in respect. Conversely, at a coronation or after Covid restrictions were lifted, or when a notable event in national or local life is to be marked, they declare the good news and, like it or not, everyone hears.

Bells summon the community to church. Sometimes this is out of public duty. At a wedding, for example, when anyone 'who knows just cause or impediment' should attend, the bells summon those whose local knowledge or objection could prevent an illegal union!

Doggerel as Woodward's rhyme may be, the chiming of his steeple bells, swung in joy at Christ's birth, is no trivial matter. Like John Betjeman, who used the phrase as the title of his 1960 autobiographical poem, we are all 'summoned by bells'. And the bells ring out peace and praise, glory and grace as they call us to worship at the cradle of salvation, the manger of Bethlehem.

Gracious Father, as heaven rings with angelic praise in celebration of the birth of your Son, our Lord Jesus Christ, may we also tell of your glory this Christmastide, as we sing 'Hosanna', in steeple, street or shop, for you reign in every place, Father, Son and Holy Spirit, in triune harmony and unison. Amen.

5 REPEAT THE SOUNDING JOY

Joy to the world!

Joy to the world, the Lord
   is come!
Let earth receive her king!
Let every heart prepare him room,
and heaven and nature sing,
and heaven and nature sing,
and heaven, and heaven and
   nature sing.

Joy to the earth, the Saviour reigns!
Let men their songs employ;
while fields and floods, rocks, hills
   and plains
repeat the sounding joy,
repeat the sounding joy,
repeat, repeat the sounding joy.

No more let sins and sorrows grow,
nor thorns infest the ground;
he comes to make his
    blessings flow
far as the curse is found,
far as the curse is found,
far as, far as the curse is found.

He rules the world with truth
    and grace,
and makes the nations prove
the glories of his righteousness
and wonders of his love,
and wonders of his love,
and wonders, wonders of his love.

Words: Isaac Watts (1674–1748)
Music: 'Antioch', Lowell Mason (1792–1872)

This is an example of a hymn that has become a Christmas carol through its use during the season of Advent, and the reasons probably lie in the first line and the exuberant tune.

A paraphrase of the second part of Psalm 98, the hymn was written by Isaac Watts, who entitled it 'The Messiah's Coming and Kingdom' and published it in *The Psalms of David: Imitated in the language of the New Testament, and applied to the Christian state and worship* in 1719. Various versions have evolved with slightly differing words, used in different regions and lands. The third verse is often omitted, yet it reminds us of its psalmic origin and is reminiscent of Isaiah 55:13, in which we are reminded that God offers blessing in response to suffering and sin. Watts described this blend of judgement and truth when he wrote: 'In [this hymn] which I formed out of the 98th Psalm I have fully expressed what I esteem to be the first and chief sense of the holy scriptures, both in this and the 96th Psalm, whose conclusions are both alike.'

The kingship referred to in the hymn can be thought of as God's or Christ's. It is more appropriate as an Advent hymn, rather than a Christmas carol, because it can more easily be associated with the second coming. It glorifies the *parousia* rather than celebrating the nativity. In this there are affinities with the great Advent hymn 'O come, O come, Emmanuel', which has also become thought of as a Christmas carol and played on the airwaves throughout December despite it being more about the return of Christ than the incarnation. By turning both hymns into Christmas carols, their origin and meaning has to some extent been diluted. Strictly speaking, 'Joy to the world!' is not a Christmas carol and should not be sung on Christmas Day.

It is good to reflect on the second coming as we head towards Christmas, and Advent hymns such as 'Joy to the world!' help us to do so. Since we tend to sing Christmas carols in the 'run-up to Christmas' now, it is serendipitous that Christmas carols that are, in fact, Advent hymns are sung during Advent, almost accidentally! 'Joy to the world!' also reminds us that Advent is not a miserable time to sing only dirges, but is rather a season in which we joyfully and expectantly look forward to the end times, when all creation shall be redeemed as Christ returns in glory (see Romans 8:18–21).

This is brought home in the hymn's third verse, which refers to the 'curse' found in Genesis 3:17–18: 'Because you have… eaten of the tree about which I commanded you, "You shall not eat of it," cursed is the ground because of you; in toil you shall eat of it all the days of your life; thorns and thistles it shall bring forth for you; and you shall eat the plants of the field.' The fall brings a curse which is only ultimately released and redeemed in the birth (and death and resurrection) of Christ. Ironically, it is this verse, which alludes to the true meaning of Christmas, that is often omitted at carol services.

The text of the hymn resonates with a modern Christmas. The idea of preparing room is something we all try to do in this season. Advent is the time of preparation – preparing to meet judgement is a classical Advent theme – but add Christmas seasoning and we can think of preparing to welcome – to make room for – the babe of Bethlehem. Christmas can be so action-packed that it becomes too easy to marginalise or forget the true meaning and purpose of Christmas as we hang up decorations, do the Christmas shopping, stock up and generally anticipate the holiday. Heaven and nature sing for joy, and amid the stresses and (in the northern hemisphere) gloomy weather, and of course the celebrations, we too can sing and 'employ our songs' in harmony with all creation.

Some people believe that George Frideric Handel wrote the tune. This is extremely unlikely, despite the fact that Lowell Mason claimed it was 'arranged from Handel' in his *Occasional Psalm and Hymn Tunes* (published in 1837), in which the tune 'Antioch' appeared. Mason preferred anonymity: an earlier collection of his anonymously published tunes sold 50,000 copies. Working for a bank at the time, he did not want his musical interests to become too well-known, so he likely attributed his own work to more famous composers. Mason was an organist at two churches in Boston, while still working as a teller at the American Bank. In 1827 he became president of the Boston Handel and Haydn Society. He was also the first music teacher in an American state-run school, and in 1833 helped found the Boston Academy of Music.

Any reservations or confusion we might have about the seasonality of the text are outweighed by the jolly tune, the mood of which manifests a sheer joyfulness that could never be inappropriate when extolling the wonder of incarnation. We can 'repeat the sounding joy', and Mason's tune literally makes us do that as we celebrate the wonders of both the first coming of truth and grace revealed in Jesus Christ and the eventual return of the Saviour. May that joy and wonder be ours every day this Advent as we journey towards Christmas.

God our king, you rule the world with truth and grace and by your Spirit bring joy to the world each day. Help us prepare a room in our hearts this Christmas, and pour down your blessings on all nations so that we may join with all creation in singing of your wondrous love made real in the incarnation of Jesus Christ our Lord. Amen.

6 O HOW BLEST THAT WONDROUS BIRTHDAY

Of the Father's heart begotten

Of the Father's heart
begotten
ere the world from chaos rose,
he is Alpha: from that Fountain,
all that is and hath been flows;
he is Omega, of all things
yet to come the mystic close,
evermore and evermore.

By his word was all created;
he commanded and 'twas done;
earth and sky and boundless ocean,
universe of three in one,
all that sees the moon's
soft radiance,
all that breathes beneath the sun,
evermore and evermore.

He assumed this mortal body,
frail and feeble, doomed to die,
that the race from dust created
might not perish utterly,
which the dreadful law
   had sentenced
in the depths of hell to lie,
   evermore and evermore.

O how blest that wondrous birthday,
when the maid the curse retrieved,
brought to birth mankind's
   salvation,
by the Holy Ghost conceived,
and the Babe, the world's redeemer,
in her loving arms received,
   evermore and evermore.

This is he, whom seer and sybil
sang in ages long gone by;
this is he of old revealèd
in the page of prophecy;
lo! he comes, the promised Saviour;
let the world his praises cry,
   evermore and evermore.

Let the storm and summer sunshine,
gliding stream and sounding shore,
sea and forest, frost and zephyr,
day and night their Lord adore;
let creation join to laud thee
through the ages evermore,
   evermore and evermore.

Sing, ye heights of heaven, his praises;
angels and archangels, sing!
wheresoe'er ye be, ye faithful,
let your joyous anthems ring,
every tongue his name confessing,
countless voices answering,
    evermore and evermore.

Words: Marcus Aurelius Clemens Prudentius (348–c. 413), translated by Roby F. Davis (1866–1937)

Music: 'Corde natus ex parentis' (mode vi), 'Divinum mysterium', *Piae Cantiones*, compiled 1582 by Theodoric Petri of Nyland (c. 1560–1630)

Originally written around the year 400, 'Of the Father's heart begotten' has a ring of ancient truth to it that also gives a flavour of early church doctrine, assimilation and attitude. The first record of Roman celebration of Christmas on 25 December dates from 336. This was one of the first Christmas hymns to be written and amazingly is still in use, occupying a major place in our seasonal liturgical celebrations, often used in processions at carol services during Advent.

Prudentius, although Spanish, wrote in Latin. A lawyer and provincial governor, he retired aged 57 and began to compose poetry and hymns, saying, 'Fail not each night in songs to celebrate the Lord.' The National Library of France holds a sixth-century copy of his *Hymnus Omnis Horae* (*Hymns for All Hours*), in which we find evidence that he intended his poems to be sung. The fourth verse of the ninth hymn is recognisable as the precursor of our hymn. In the first verse, he simply used 'A and O' to signify the first and last letters of the Greek alphabet (see Revelation 22:13), and they scan as single syllables:

> *Corde natus ex Parentis ante mundi exordium,*
> *Al -ph'et O(mega) cognominatus, ipse fons et clausula*
> *Omnium quae sunt fuerunt, quaeque post futura sunt.*

A manuscript in St Gallen in Switzerland dates from between 1034 and 1047, as does one from Exeter as well as in breviaries (liturgical prayer books) from York and Hereford. Around this time the refrain '*Saeculorum saeculis*' ('Evermore and evermore') crept in from a different part of the longer poem. As an 'office hymn', it was stipulated to be sung for services of worship at set hours. Examples of its use were at the vespers of St Stephen's Day (26 December) and services of compline (night prayer) in the eight days after Christmas.

The tune originally sung is not what we use today, even though the origins of the modern tune are medieval. The plainsong journey began when Prudentius' words were inserted into a singing of the *Sanctus* ('Holy, Holy') during the Eucharist. Modern hymn books, not least the *Revised English Hymnal* (2023), still print an adapted plainsong tune, but the tune 'Divinum mysterium' is used more often, especially at carol services. Given the ancient origins of both tune and text, it is no surprise that versions and variations of both proliferate, even to the point of a different opening line – 'Of the Father's *love* begotten' in some books.

Leaving the history and musicology behind, we can consider what this hymn tells us. It is an early exposition of the true meaning and theology of Christmas: before anything was created, God was, the beginning and the end (first verse). As the gospel of John puts it: 'All things came into being through him, and without him not one thing came into being' (John 1:3), for 'In the beginning when God created the heavens and the earth, the earth was a formless void' (Genesis 1:1, NRSVA).

The second verse goes on to remind us that 'God said, "Let there be light," and there was light' (Genesis 1:3), for 'In the beginning was the Word, and the Word was with God, and the Word was God' (John 1:1). The 'universe of three in one' reminds us that God is Trinity, inseparable, and that what the Father does by word, in the Word and by the Spirit who moves upon the waters (Genesis 1:2) and at Pentecost (Acts 2:2), is indivisible. For Christ 'is the image of the invisible God, the firstborn of all creation, for in him all things in heaven and on earth were created' (Colossians 1:15–16).

The third verse brings us to incarnation, as Jesus, 'though he was in the form of God, did not regard equality with God as something to be exploited, but… being born in human likeness… and being found in human form' (Philippians 2:6–8, NRSVA) lived and went about among us. This he did to cancel the curse put on Adam, 'a pattern of the one who was to come' (Romans 5:14), whose original sin led to the human condition whereby 'you are dust, and to dust you shall return' (Genesis 3:19). Such is the law of God, that sin condemns us all, as 'death came through sin, and so death spread to all because all have sinned' (Romans 5:12).

This release from the consequences of sin is what makes the birthday of Jesus so 'wondrous', as the fourth verse puts it. The 'maid', the virgin Mary, 'retrieves' the curse by giving birth to and caring for the sinless one, who died for the ungodly (Romans 5:6), to take away the sins of the world (John 1:29). As Paul wrote: 'Therefore just as one man's trespass led to condemnation for all, so one man's act of righteousness leads to justification and life for all' (Romans 5:18).

As the hymn continues we hear of the 'seer and sybil', the latter of which, being ancient Greek prophetesses, were translated by John Mason Neale as 'sages'. Nonetheless, there were some pagan sybils whose prophecies were associated with the coming of a saviour. Prudentius would have known of the Cumaean sibyl, who in Virgil's *Fourth Eclogue* foretells the coming of a saviour. Later Christian writers identified this as Christ. Meanwhile, the oracle at Delphi was a priestess of Apollo, called Pythia, who answered questions about the future. In Acts 16:16–18 Paul and Silas encounter a female slave who has 'a spirit of divination' or, in the original New Testament Greek, 'a spirit of Python', which reminds us of the sibyl of Delphi and the cult of Apollo. She proclaims them as servants of the most high God, and while Paul challenges the cult of Apollo he turns a sibyl into a sort of Christian prophet.

Another sibyl, the Samian sibyl, presided over the Apollonian oracle near the temple of Hera on Samos. She is said to have prophesied the birth of Jesus in the stable. Another story which Prudentius may have known concerns the Tiburtine sibyl, who predicted the coming of a final emperor named Constans, who would defeat the enemies of Christianity, ending paganism. (Constantine did indeed initiate the Christianisation of the Roman empire.) These and other sibyls feature in the classical world of mythology, known to Christians and to some extent adopted by them. As far as the fifth verse of the hymn is concerned, Prudentius is drawing on a rich vein of Jewish and classical prophecy pointing to Christ's birth.

The next verse introduces another classical creation, the zephyr. He was the personified God of the west wind, the most gentle and favourable. Notwithstanding this pagan origin, here the zephyr is a western breeze, which like the seas and skies join in adoration of God. The final verse of praise extols not only all creation, but also all heaven, to praise God for his wondrous work of incarnation and salvation. May we all continue to do that evermore and evermore!

Before all things you are God. By your eternal spirit,
sustain our worship, that through prophecy and praise,
we may always sing of the redemption you have sent
us in your Son, Jesus Christ our Lord. Amen.

7 WHAT CAN I GIVE HIM?

In the bleak midwinter

In the bleak midwinter, frosty wind made moan,
earth stood hard as iron, water like a stone;
snow had fallen, snow on snow, snow on snow,
in the bleak midwinter, long ago.

Our God, heaven cannot hold him, nor earth sustain;
heaven and earth shall flee away when he comes to reign.
In the bleak midwinter a stable place sufficed
the Lord God Almighty, Jesus Christ.

Enough for him, whom cherubim, worship night and day,
a breastful of milk, and a mangerful of hay;
enough for him, whom angels fall before,
the ox and ass and camel which adore.

Angels and archangels may have gathered there,
cherubim and seraphim thronged the air;
but his mother only, in her maiden bliss,
worshipped the beloved with a kiss.

What can I give him, poor as I am?
If I were a shepherd, I would bring a lamb;
if I were a wise man, I would do my part;
yet what I can I give him: give my heart.

Words: Christina Rossetti (1830–94)

Music: 'Cranham', Gustav Theodore Holst (1874–1934); Harold Darke (1888–1976)

While others may have topped the Christmas carol charts, this Christmas poem – and its two fine musical accompaniments – is the favourite of many. Some love Gustav Holst's tune, while others prefer the choral setting by Harold Darke.

Gustav Holst was born in Cheltenham with German, Scandinavian and Russian heritage. From 1905 he was director of music at St Paul's Girls' School in Hammersmith. A trombonist, Holst developed an interest in other religions and cultures and made his own translations of Sanskrit for his *Choral Hymns from the Rig Veda*. His fascination for mysticism is reflected not only in parts of 'The Planets' but also in the 'Ode to Death' and the 'Hymn of Jesus', the latter of which opens with the plainchant 'Pange lingua'.

Harold Darke was an organist at St Michael's, Cornhill in the City of London from 1916 to 1966, and he also covered at King's College, Cambridge while Boris Ord was called up. He is most known in Anglican musical circles for his Communion settings and for this sublime setting of Rossetti's poem, which many prefer to Holst's, but which omits the fourth verse.

Christina Rossetti's 'A Christmas carol' was first published in *Scribner's Monthly* in January 1872. The irregularities of the metre might indicate that she never actually expected it to be sung, nor did she hear it sung, for it was not until 1906 that it was published with Holst's tune in the *English Hymnal*. We have learnt where to add or omit notes accordingly, as each verse is slightly different melodically.

Christina Rossetti's father was a refugee from Naples who was professor of Italian at King's College, London. According to her brother, she composed her first poem before she was able to write. She is often considered to be a melancholic character, but he described her as vivacious at first. They were an intellectual family of four children, who abandoned an evangelical leaning for Anglo-Catholicism. In 1854 she volunteered to assist Florence Nightingale in the Crimean War effort, but was rejected. Her poems began to appear in print from 1862.

In the early 1870s she contracted Graves' disease and was dangerously ill. Her commitment to Anglo-Catholicism strengthened, however, and she became outspoken politically against slavery, imperialism, military aggression and animal experimentation. In the 1890s she wrote a commentary on the book of Revelation. At home in 1892 she underwent a mastectomy due to breast cancer, but to little avail: she suffered terribly until her death on 29 December 1894. The Anglican Church commemorates her on 27 April.

Her poem has three main aspects which make it a hit: sentimentality, Englishness and theology. The first verse sets the scene, not in first-century Jerusalem but in chilly Britain: pure, holy white snow carpets the English rock-hard soil. Blended with bleakness is sentimentality: the humble stable occupied by oxen, donkeys and camels (there is no biblical warrant for placing these animals in the house where

Jesus was born!). Angels and animals worship the child at the breast. Mary provides sustenance and comfort, and the simplest gift of a kiss. It is idealised and human, transcending place and time and language and involves universal imagery.

The notion that God needs to take on human flesh, to come to earth as Emmanuel – God among us – suggests a breaking free, an imperative to save. The idea of heaven and earth fleeing, resonates with Revelation 21:1: 'Then I saw a new heaven and a new earth, for the first heaven and the first earth had passed away, and the sea was no more.' Rossetti links the first coming with the second, such that the babe of Bethlehem is a sign of the end times too. The angels worship continually, also echoing Revelation: 'Day and night without ceasing they sing, "Holy, holy, holy, the Lord God the Almighty, who was and is and is to come."' (Revelation 4:8). Yet there is a juxtaposition of human and divine, not only in the Christ-child himself but in the surroundings: heavenly angels above; hay and milk below.

Finally Rosetti unleashes the spiritual bombshell which has wrapped up Christmas history, sentimentality and theology in one profound but simple package. To the Lamb of God, the shepherds bring a baby sheep. The magi bring symbolic and wealthy gifts. And all of these locate the hymn in the biblical story. Nevertheless, we can do something which transcends time and place, we can offer ourselves: our worship, in spirit and in truth, from the heart. The gift that is God comes from God, unwarranted, unprompted, the gift of God's very self to a fallen humanity. God gives me himself; I give him myself.

O God, whom heaven cannot hold, you came to the bleak midwinter of our world and gave us the gift of yourself, in fragile, frail form. Nurtured by his mother and worshipped by saints and angels, may we too join with all creation in offering ourselves in service to the one who is Prince of Peace and Lamb of God, even Jesus Christ our Lord. Amen.

8 ALL IN WHITE SHALL WAIT AROUND

Once in royal David's city

Once in royal David's city
stood a lowly cattle shed,
where a mother laid her baby
in a manger for his bed:
Mary was the mother mild,
Jesus Christ her little child.

He came down to earth
from heaven
who is God and Lord of all,
and his shelter was a stable,
and his cradle was a stall:
with the poor and mean and lowly
lived on earth our Saviour holy.

And through all his wondrous
    childhood
he would honour and obey,
love and watch the lowly maiden,
in whose gentle arms he lay:
Christian children all must be
mild, obedient, good as he.

For he is our childhood's pattern,
day by day like us he grew,
he was little, weak and helpless,
tears and smiles like us he knew;
and he feeleth for our sadness,
and he shareth in our gladness.

And our eyes at last shall see him,
through his own redeeming love,
for that child so dear and gentle
is our Lord in heaven above;
and he leads his children on
to the place where he is gone.

Not in that poor lowly stable,
with the oxen standing by,
we shall see him; but in heaven,
set at God's right hand on high;
where like stars, his children
    crowned
all in white shall wait around.

Words: Cecil Frances Alexander (1818–95)
Music: 'Irby', Henry J. Gauntlett (1805–76)

This popular and evocative Christmas hymn was penned by a woman who wanted to teach children the truths of the gospel as expressed in the creed. Fanny Humphries wrote most of her hymns before marrying William Alexander in 1850. He was an Irish Anglican, sometime bishop of Derry and Raphoe from 1867, who became Archbishop of Armagh after her death. She gave away to charity almost all the money she earned from writing, helping to establish an institute for the deaf in Strabane, Northern Ireland. On the day of her funeral, in October 1885, the shops were closed, 92 clergymen attended and the streets of Londonderry were full of mourners, such was the affection in which she was held.

'Once in royal David's city', along with 'There is a green hill far away' and 'All things bright and beautiful', were published in her 1848 booklet, *Hymns for Little Children*, 41 hymns set out to explain the catechism and the tenets of the Creed in memorable verse. 'Once in royal David's city' was about the virgin birth; 'There is a green hill', the passion of Christ; and 'All things bright and beautiful' praised God as creator. The other hymns have fallen out of use, being very much a product of the language, outlook and attitude of their day. The idea that 'Christian children all must be, mild, obedient, good as he' rankles with some worshippers, as such sentiments are redolent of the Victorian Sunday school with its dry and disciplined biblical learning.

Yet Alexander was trying to help by writing singable hymns which conveyed essential Christian truths. In writing 'Once in royal David's city', she demonstrated both her love of children and her understanding of the humanity of Christ. Like many youth workers since, her heart was very much in the mission and evangelisation of young people, always striving to bring the gospel up to date for each and every generation.

'Irby', the tune invariably used, was composed by Henry Gauntlett for these words, and the hymn as we know it first appeared in 1849 and made it into the first edition of *Hymns Ancient and Modern* in 1861. It is not clear why the tune was called 'Irby', as Gauntlett does not seem to have had any link with any of the three English towns of that name. For many this hymn and tune are the archetypal commencement of a carol service, sung by a lone chorister, usually a child.

It is easy to forget that when 'Once in royal David's city' was written, up to half of recorded deaths were of children under the age of five. In 1848, the same year she wrote the hymn, Fanny Humphries also published 'The Lord of the forest and his vassals', a story dedicated 'to her little cousins to help them become "little Christians"'. In that story she writes of 'A shorter grave at their feet where the white-robed children often come, to dress the turf with flowers, and talk, with tears and smiles, of the happy little children.' We cannot help but be reminded of 'Where like stars, his children crowned, all in white shall wait around'. To those many parents who had lost little ones, these words provided some comfort, that those brief lives were not lost to God.

While the first verse tells of Christ's birth in straightforward terms, the second verse introduces a reference to the Christ we encounter in Philippians 2:6–7: 'Who, though he existed in the form of God, did not regard equality with God as something to be grasped, but emptied himself, taking the form of a slave, assuming human likeness.' The verse goes on to remind us of Christ's earthly poverty, as referred to in 2 Corinthians 8:9: 'Though he was rich, yet for your sakes he became poor, so that by his poverty you might become rich.'

The next verse reminds us of Jesus' sinlessness, as set out in 1 John 3:5: 'You know that he was revealed to take away sins, and in him there is no sin.' Though sinless, he was also human; like us, he knew of the joys and pains ('tears and smiles') of human existence, and this is touched upon in the fourth verse. The fifth verse reminds us of the end of the story: of Christ risen, ascended, glorified. Christ reigning in heaven is not a childish fantasy, but a scriptural truth. 'All in white, waiting around' describes those who have their robes washed in the blood of the lamb (Revelation 4:4; 7:14), as well as comforting those who have lost children. Firmly rooted in the earthbound stable, we look upwards to that higher, purer place, where there will be no more tears: a new heaven and earth, presided over by our Lord Jesus Christ (Revelation 21:1–4).

Father God, whose son Jesus Christ came down to earth from heaven, hear our prayers for all who are weak and helpless, and by the power of your redeeming love, lead us your children to share in the gladness of that day when all tears shall be turned to smiles in your heavenly city, where with saints and angels attending, you reign in glory forever. Amen.

9 REJOICE YE VALES AND MOUNTAINS

A great and mighty wonder

A great and mighty wonder,
a full and holy cure!
the Virgin bears the Infant
with virgin-honour pure:

Repeat the hymn again:
'To God on high be glory,
and peace on earth to men.'

The Word becomes incarnate,
and yet remains on high;
and cherubim sing anthems
to shepherds from the sky:

While thus they sing your Monarch,	Since all he comes to ransom,
those bright angelic bands,	by all be he adored,
rejoice, ye vales and mountains,	the infant born in Bethl'em,
ye oceans, clap your hands:	the Saviour and the Lord:

Words: 'Mega kai paradoxon thauma tetelestai', St Germanus of Constantinople (c. 634–732), translated by John Mason Neale (1818–66)

Music: 'Es ist ein ros entsprungen', German carol melody harmonised by Michael Praetorius (1571–1621)

As we get closer to Christmas our attention begins to turn from the second coming (the theme of Advent) towards the first coming, the incarnation. This ancient hymn is thoroughly incarnational, with verses that resonate well with the idea we find in John's gospel, that in the holy birth at Bethlehem, 'God is with us'. This contrasts with the focus on babyhood, festivity, the meekness and mildness of the cosy, smiling virgin, the pastoral idyll of shepherds in the field, and the domestic bliss at the crib. The two dimensions are blended in a modern Christmas, and they now seem to be as connected as the dual nature of incarnation itself. Just as we have learnt to sing in two contrasting but complementary December languages, Christmas is a time to have fun and a time to be serious – a time to celebrate and try to exemplify goodwill, but also a time to reflect upon the realities of sin, the need for redemption and the extreme lengths and great cost to which God, Father, Son and Holy Spirit, went to bring it all about.

The second line, 'a full and holy cure', seems a little obscure now, but relates to the curing of the sickness of sin, which the virgin birth 'heals' through immaculate conception. The sinfulness of humankind is 'cured' by the fact that Jesus is born without sin, to take away the sins of the world, through atoning death and resurrection. The refrain is a reference to the 'Gloria' (Luke 2:14) and stands very much in the tradition of the use of those lines ('*Gloria in excelsis Deo*') in several other Christmas hymns, although here it is not in Latin.

Verse two reminds us of the paradox of incarnation: that God is on earth among us, but is also on high, Father and Son. In Greek it is called the *homousios*, denoting the distinctive and unique inseparability we find in the Godhead. Jesus is both God and human being, also effectively in two 'places' at once. Meanwhile, as in the refrain, the angels bring heavenly praise down to earthly and earthy shepherds. There is a reference to Psalm 98:7–8: 'Let the sea roar and all that fills it, the world and those who live in it. Let the floods clap their hands; let the hills sing together for joy.' The final verse quotes Mark 10:45: 'For the Son of Man came not to be served but to serve and to give his life a ransom for many.'

As with many Christmas hymns, the connection between the crib and the cross is made, as incarnation is not simply a theological way of interpreting the nativity, but an overarching systematic theology of how the baby in the manger is the Saviour of the world. He is this Saviour through being not only divine and human, but also integrally and eternally consubstantiated in the Holy Trinity of Father, Son and Holy Spirit.

The composer of this hymn's sublime tune, Michael Praetorius, is believed to have died on his 50th birthday in 1621. He was born in Creuzburg, which is on the Werra River near Eisenach in Germany: the town so often associated with Martin Luther (1483–1546) and J.S. Bach (1685–1750), both of whom attended the Lateinschule there, albeit nearly 200 years apart. The young Michael studied there too, where his father (also called Michael) taught. One of his colleagues was Johann Walter (1496–1570), who had worked with Luther on his first collection of chorales in 1524. So the school, which Luther described as 'like purgatory and hell', and at which J.S. Bach had a poor attendance record despite singing well, also has a connection with the Praetorius family.

There is more: Michael Praetorius Senior studied with Luther and Melanchthon (Luther's biographer) in Wittenberg and, on becoming a pastor, was put in charge of Creuzberg, where his son was born. Being strict Lutherans – dissenting Protestants effectively – his father was frequently sacked. In 1582 Michael Junior matriculated at Frankfurt University, where his brother was professor of theology. He developed an interest in and knowledge of Protestant hymnody while there, and in the late 1580s became organist at St Marien, Frankfurt, the university and parish church. He wrote *Syntagma Musicum* (1614–20), an important musicological book which contains not only detailed information about late 16th- and early 17th-century music, but also a section on the musical instruments of his day.

Praetorius stands firmly in the chronological and musical space between Luther and Bach, being a theologically minded musicologist, and he can be credited with the establishment and maintenance of a long tradition of Lutheran chorale and Mass music, while also giving that tradition sufficient flexibility to grow and adapt. Lutheran music owes this largely self-taught musician a huge debt, even if he is overlooked today.

This chorale arrangement of a folk carol originating in 15th- or early 16th-century Trier, *Es ist ein ros enstsprungen* appears in many hymn books, usually as 'A great and mighty wonder', which is a much older poem from the seventh century. Originally written by St Germanus, the version we know was translated by the prolific Victorian hymnwriter and translator John Mason Neale. Germanus' father was executed as a traitor, which meant that poor Germanus was castrated and put in the care of the clergy at Hagia Sophia in Constantinople (now Istanbul), where he studied theology. He was appointed bishop of Cyzicus sometime around 706 and became patriarch of Constantinople in 715. He was forced to resign 15 years later under pressure from

Pope Leo III, and the various heretical controversies which surrounded him prompted him to retire to Athens. His most significant claim to fame now is this hymn.

Neale's translation of it appeared in his *Hymns of the Eastern Church* in 1862, in which he wrongly ascribed it to St Anatolius. Meanwhile, it is not Neale's unadulterated text which we have today: the editors of *English Hymnal* (1906) altered his six four-line verses and created a refrain – 'Repeat the hymn again: "To God on high be glory, and peace on earth to men."'

This deeply meaningful incarnational hymn is not often sung by the congregation at carol services, being elbowed out by the bigger blockbusters, but often finds a place as a choir carol, not least because of the ethereal beauty of the music. A particularly evocative modern German version is by Jan Sandstrom.

O God and Father of our Lord Jesus Christ, as we repeat the songs of Christmas again, help us remember the great cost of salvation and the complexities of incarnation by which we have been redeemed. As we reflect on these great and mighty wonders, bring heaven to earth that our earthbound praise and prayers may rise to your throne. Amen.

10 LET US ALL WITH ONE ACCORD

The first Nowell

The first Nowell the angel did say
was to three poor shepherds in
fields as they lay,
in fields where they lay keeping
their sheep,
in a cold winter's night that was
so deep.

Nowell, Nowell, Nowell, Nowell,
born is the king of Israel.

They lookéd up and saw a star
shining in the east, beyond them far,
and to the earth it gave great light,
and so it continued, both day
and night.

And by the light of that same star
three wise men came from country far,
to seek for a king was their intent,
and to follow the star wherever it went.

This star drew nigh to the
    north-west;
o'er Bethlehem it took its rest.
And there it did both stop and stay,
right over the place where Jesus lay.

Then did they know assuredly
within that house, the king did lie;
one entered in then for to see
and found the babe in poverty.

Then enter'd in those wise
    men three,
full reverently upon their knee,
and offer'd there in his presence,
their gold, and myrrh, and
    frankincense.

Between an ox stall and an ass,
this child truly there born he was;
for want of clothing they did him lay
all in a manger, among the hay.

Then let us all with one accord
sing praises to our heavenly Lord;
that hath made heaven and earth
    of nought,
and with his blood mankind
    hath bought.

If we in our time shall do well,
we shall be free from death and hell,
for God hath prepared for us all
a resting place in general.

Words: Cornish carol, c. 18th century

Music: 'The first Nowell', English traditional, arranged by John Stainer (1840–1901)

Christmas is about mystery, the great mystery of incarnation. Some carols reflect on this; others try to express it. This carol models it! First, what on earth (or in heaven) does 'Nowell' mean? In French, and sometimes in English, it is *Noël*. We can track the word through Latin and Old French's *Nouel* to Middle English as *nowel*. In 1823 it gained a second 'l'. The Latin derivation is said to be *natalis*, relating to birth; thus in Italian, we say '*Buon natale*' for 'Happy Christmas'. In French 'Happy Birthday' is '*Joyeux anniversaire*' and in Italian '*Buon compleanno*'. In Germanic languages, the emphasis remains on birth, as in '*Alles Gute zum Geburtstag*'.

The key here is that in Latin-based languages, the *natalis* refers not simply to a birthday, but to *the* birthday: the birthday above all birthdays – the birthday of our Lord. In English, again drawing on the Latin origins, we speak of the nativity. Because English as we now use it has is origins both in Germanic and Latin languages (Danish and Norman French specifically), we have a significant etymological heritage and a wide vocabulary.

Some people believe that 'Nowell' has something to do with novelty, lining it to *novellare* (Latin) and *nouvelle* (French), with the implication that it is an exclamation of 'News! News!' This we find, for example, in some versions of the first verse of 'Good Christian men rejoice' (*In Dulci Jubilo*): 'News! News! Jesus Christ is born today!' This is likely coincidental and does not represent a literal translation of either the German or Latin in which that carol was originally composed in the early 14th century. However, the idea that Jesus' birth is news is a good one. It is, in the true spirit of 'gospel', good news, the greatest news hailing the beginning of the greatest story ever told. This undertone of news makes far better sense than some older versions of 'The first Nowell' which replace the key word with 'O well'!

The biblical account of the angel's 'first nowell' says: 'I am bringing you good news of great joy for all the people: to you is born this day in the city of David a Saviour, who is the Messiah, the Lord' (Luke 2:10–12). Here we have birth *and* good news! A single angel proclaims this, and the hosts of angels then say, 'Glory to God in the highest heaven' (Luke 2:14). Whoever wrote 'The first Nowell' knew the Bible well, and they did not fall into the trap of assuming that the angels *sang*, nor overlooked the 'one angel then all' approach that the shepherds experienced. Some printings slip up on this however, attributing 'nowell' to the whole throng: 'the angels did say'.

The carol relates the nativity story, from Christmas Eve to Epiphany. Most versions omit verses 5, 7 and 9, which both shortens it (it is long and repetitive enough with six) and removes the last verse which refers to death and hell rather awkwardly and concludes with the infelicitous rhyme of 'all' and 'general'. The complete text was published by the lawyer-musician William Sandys in a book of 80 carols called *Christmas Carols, Ancient and Modern*, published in 1833. This volume gives us versions of 'A virgin unspotted', 'God rest you merry, gentlemen' and 'The Cherry Tree

Carol', and Sandys' name is enshrined in the name of the tune for George Herbert's hymn 'Teach me, my God and king'. The Cornish origin of the text can be traced to the 15th century, through 18th-century publications, and appeared a decade before Sandys published it in an edition by Davies Gilbert, who sourced it from Helston, and a manuscript dated 1816, which is stored in the County Record office in Truro.

A deeper mystery surrounding 'The first Nowell' concerns the tune. Sandys provided one, which he had collected in 1827, but what we sing now is an arrangement made in 1871 by the great Victorian organist Sir John Stainer for *Christmas Carols, New and Old*. Even such a pedigree cannot disguise the fundamentally repetitive nature of the tune. Some editors have suggested that the transcriber was not paying attention or forgot part of it, or more interestingly that the fact that the thrice-repeated line ends on the mediant (third note of the scale) suggests that it may not have been meant to have been the tune at all. Instead, it might be a harmony part, a kind of descant, possibly even to another tune from Cambourne, also in Cornwall.

Such speculation is fraught with difficulty, because a part of the Cambourne tune also resonates rather well with the Sussex Carol ('On Christmas night all Christians sing'). Just as we might say of two tunes to 'Away in a manger' ('Mueller' and 'Cradle song'), they may 'fit' or 'work' together, being singable simultaneously, but this does not mean they were meant to. In that period, carol singers, often as children, did not generally 'read' music but learnt it by ear, and up in the church's west gallery, from where such carols were often sung, errors and hybrid versions could easily occur and evolve. West gallery musicians were notoriously unruly and ill-disciplined, inclined to 'do their own thing', sometimes to the great annoyance and frustration of the clergy! In the 18th century, John Brown, vicar of Newcastle, wrote:

> In country churches, wherever a more artificial kind of music hath been imprudently attempted, confusion and dissonance are the general consequence.

Some carols were sung in pubs (particularly in Yorkshire), also leading to proliferation and variation, as much through circumstance as intention. When it comes to 'The first Nowell', it seems likely that the tune we sing now is a hybrid of the tenor (middle) part and the treble (upper) line of a carol that was invariably sung from memory by those who might not have learnt the same version as everyone else!

The greater mystery is incarnation itself. For just as melodies weave their way through history, perhaps misunderstood, repeated incorrectly, altered deliberately or accidently, so too can the story be misshaped by time and error. Throughout theological history, the idea that at Christmas the Word became flesh – that Jesus Christ, the babe of Bethlehem and crucified Lord, is both God and man – has been buffeted by the winds of heresy. What emerges (and there is no space here to go into detail) are hybrid versions of faith and doctrine, which at times have captured the imagination and commitment of groups of Christians. Reformations have focused on reclaiming or correcting error or recasting new ecclesiastical structures, and there have been many descants to the main melody of the mystery that is the incarnation.

Sometimes the tune is lost, irretrievably perhaps, yet underneath, the melody of love and harmony of truth prevails even if one has to listen hard to hear it. This is true at Christmas, when the basic story may be submerged by the descants of frivolity, or it may be true of the principal doctrines of the church as side issues cloud the truth that 'God so loved the world that he gave his only Son, so that everyone who believes in him may not perish but may have eternal life' (John 3:16). That is the true meaning of 'Nowell'.

God, amid the multiple lines of theory and polemic,
hold before us the great mystery of incarnation, so
that we may know assuredly the costly gift of the Word
made flesh, which the angels proclaimed and which
you have given us in Jesus Christ our Lord. Amen.

11 EVERY KNEE SHALL THEN BOW DOWN

Angels from the realms of glory

Angels from the realms
of glory,
wing your flight o'er all the earth;
ye who sang creation's story
now proclaim Messiah's birth.

Come and worship,
worship Christ, the newborn king
        or
Gloria, in excelsis Deo

Shepherds, in the field abiding,
watching o'er your flocks by night,
God with man is now residing;
yonder shines the infant light.

Sages, leave your contemplations,
brighter visions beam afar;
seek the great Desire of Nations;
ye have seen his natal star.

Saints, before the altar bending,
watching long in hope and fear;
suddenly the Lord descending,
in his temple shall appear.

Sinners, wrung with true
    repentance,
doom'd for guilt to endless pains;
justice now revokes the sentence,
mercy calls you – break your chains.

Though an infant now we view him,
he shall fill his Father's throne;
gather all nations to him,
every knee shall then bow down.

Lord of heaven, we adore thee,
God the Father, God the Son,
God the Spirit, one in glory,
on the same eternal throne.

Words: James Montgomery (1771–1854); v. 7: Isaac Gregory Smith (1826–1920)

Music: 'Iris', French traditional, arranged by Martin Shaw (1875–1958)

This Christmas hymn, which is especially suitable for use at Communion services, has a dual identity: it can be seen as an original text by James Montgomery or as a version of an older French carol which we know as 'Angels we have heard on high'. They are substantially different, but in essence the same. A translation of the French song is as follows:

Angels we have heard on high
sweetly singing o'er the plains,
and the mountains in reply
echoing their joyous strains.
Gloria, in excelsis Deo!

Shepherds, why this jubilee?
Why your joyous strains prolong?
What the gladsome tidings be
which inspire your heavenly song?

Come to Bethlehem and see
him whose birth the angels sing;
come, adore on bended knee,
Christ the Lord, the newborn king.

See him in a manger laid,
whom the choirs of angels praise;
Mary, Joseph, lend your aid,
while our hearts in love we raise.

The metre and the tune are the same. A central verse has not been translated:

Ils annoncent la naissance
du libérateur d'Israël,
et pleins de reconnaissance
chantent en ce jour solennel.
Gloria, in excelsis Deo.

It is immediately evident that one is not a translation of the other, and the refrain of one has been used for the other. It was not an authentic thing to do, but the editors of the 1928 *Oxford Carol Book* took the 'Gloria' from the French carol and swapped it for what Montgomery had written, 'Come and worship, worship Christ, the newborn king.'

Although the French song may be older than Montgomery's text, his version has an older source. It first appeared in the *Sheffield Iris* on 24 December 1816. The tune

'Iris' is named after this first appearance. James Montgomery was an apprentice baker who preferred music and poetry and became a bookseller before taking a job as bookkeeper and clerk for *The Sheffield Register* in 1792. When his editor had to flee, as the army turned up to arrest him for supporting the French revolution, Montgomery took over and gave it a new name: *The Sheffield Iris*.

Montgomery also supported the revolutionaries, writing a poem about the fall of the Bastille in 1795, and the following year he was imprisoned in York for six months for criticising the militia's handling of a riot. He continued to edit the *Iris* through the Napoleonic Wars, finally selling the paper in 1825. The same year, in *The Christmas Box*, he published another carol 'The babe of Bethlehem', from which verse 6 above is taken, being sometimes a substitute for the stronger verse 5. Smith's alternative final verse, written in 1855, is also given above as verse 7.

The earliest reference to the song dates from 1867, in a theological dictionary which dates it only as far back as 1842. Research among French Canadians in Quebec supports this dating. Nevertheless, the tune is thought to be an 18th-century 'Noël', perhaps from Lorraine or Provence. While in relation to 'The First Nowell' we might wonder what the word means, in terms of French music, they are effectively shepherds' pipe carols, played on southern French hillsides. Hector Berlioz mimics them beautifully in his 'Thou must leave thy holy dwelling', taken from his cantata

'L'enfance du Christ', completed in 1854. The authentic ones are clearly older, such as those used by Marc-Antoine Charpentier in his 'Messe de minuit' (1694), which is full of them. Therefore the tune to 'Les anges dans nos campagnes', could well predate the publication of Montgomery's text.

Montgomery did not provide nor specify a tune. For a brief time in the USA the tune 'Cwm Rhondda' ('Guide me, O thou great redeemer') was used. It is more often sung to 'Regent Square', composed by Henry Thomas Smart (1813–79) in 1866. This tune is also used for 'Lord of glory, thine the splendour'. The editors of *The Oxford Carol Book* made the marriage with 'Iris' that has endured in the UK.

Martin Shaw was organist at St Mary's, Primrose Hill, then St Martin-in-the-Fields, and he was one of the founders of what was to become the Royal School of Church Music. Along with his brother Geoffrey Shaw, the Revd Percy Dearmer and Ralph Vaughan Williams, they were collectively responsible for *Songs of Praise* (1925, 1931) and the *Oxford Book of Carols* (1928). Shaw takes some credit for 'Morning has broken', having commissioned Eleanor Farjeon to write a text to go with a Gaelic tune ('Bunessan') which he had unearthed. 'Angels from the realms of glory' is not his greatest achievement, even if it has been significant. The union was based on the two sets of words looking the same (though some would say they do not really fit). He also made it bilingual by adding the Latin 'Gloria' from the French song. Given that Montgomery was a non-conformist revolutionary, he would likely not have approved!

At the heart of this macaronic muddle is a profound hymn. There is a verse for everyone – angels, shepherds, sages, saints and sinners. With the English refrain, we are reminded that the hymn is a call to worship and that singing the 'Gloria' after a verse about the magi does not fit with the story. Reference to kneeling at the altar gives the hymn a hint of Anglo-Catholicism, which would have been alien to Montgomery but which nevertheless turns the hymn into a devotional one. In eucharistic prayer the Lord is present in bread and wine. In this and the succeeding verse (written later) we are reminded of Paul's prophecy based on an ancient hymn:

> Therefore God exalted him even more highly
>> and gave him the name
>> that is above every other name,
> so that at the name given to Jesus
>> every knee should bend,
>> in heaven and on earth and under the earth,
> and every tongue should confess
>> that Jesus Christ is Lord,
>> to the glory of God the Father.
> PHILIPPIANS 2:9–11

Not many Christmas carols lend themselves so well to worship as 'Angels from the realms of glory'; fewer to Holy Communion. It may not have been envisaged by the author, but then much of what has transpired with this carol has not been authentic and is more a consequence of editorial decisions, trial and error. God is not deterred and still calls us daily to come and worship. That this carol has become a suitable song of summons is a serendipitous recognition of the glory of God, offered by angels, shepherds, sages, saints and sinners alike.

Jesus, whose birth we celebrate at this time, call us
your people to kneel and worship you enthroned in the
manger. Shine your infant light on this dark world of sin,
that with holiness and wisdom your people may bring
hope in the face of fear and love to all nations. Amen.

12 ON CHRISTMAS DAY IN THE MORNING

I saw three ships

I saw three ships come sailing in
On Christmas Day, on Christmas Day
I saw three ships come sailing in
On Christmas Day in the morning

And what was in those ships all three?
On Christmas Day, on Christmas Day
And what was in those ships all three?
On Christmas Day in the morning

Our Saviour Christ and his lady
On Christmas Day, on Christmas Day
Our Saviour Christ and his lady
On Christmas Day in the morning

Pray whither sailed those ships all three?
On Christmas Day, on Christmas Day
Pray whither sailed those ships all three?
On Christmas Day in the morning

Oh, they sailed into Bethlehem
On Christmas Day, on Christmas Day
Oh, they sailed into Bethlehem
On Christmas Day in the morning

And all the bells on earth shall ring
On Christmas Day, on Christmas Day
And all the bells on earth shall ring
On Christmas Day in the morning

And all the angels in heaven shall sing
On Christmas Day, on Christmas Day
And all the angels in heaven shall sing
On Christmas Day in the morning

And all the souls on earth shall sing
On Christmas Day, on Christmas Day
And all the souls on earth shall sing
On Christmas Day in the morning

Then let us all rejoice, amain
On Christmas Day, on Christmas Day
Then let us all rejoice, amain
On Christmas Day in the morning

Words: English, c. 17th century, collected by William Sandys (1792–1874)
Music: Melody from *Christmas Carols, New and Old* (1871)

This Christmas sea song first surfaced around 1666, the year of the great fire of London. In that year, Scotsman John Forbes included it in his *Cantus, Songs and Fancies to Three, Four or Five Parts*. William Sandys, who compiled *Christmas Carols, Ancient and Modern* in 1833, knew it through a book called *Scotch Songs* and quoted with it a verse with a deeper theological meaning that seems to have since been thrown overboard:

All sons of Adam, rise up with me,
Go praise the Blessed Trinitie, &c.
Then spake the Archangel Gabriel, said, Ave, Marie mild,
The Lord of Lords is with thee, now shall you go with child.
  Ecce ancilla domini.

Then said the virgin, as thou hast said, so mat it be,
  Welcome be heaven's king.
There comes a ship far sailing then,
Saint Michael was the stieres-man;
  Saint John sate in the horn:
Our Lord harped, our Lady sang,
And all the bells of heaven they rang,
  On Christ's sonday at morn, &c.

Note the presence of the archangel Michael as skipper and St John in the crew! Sandys also linked it to a different carol, a Cornish one, the first verse of which is: 'As I sat on a sunny bank (*three times*), on Christmas Day in the morning.' (See *The Cornish Song Book*, 1929). The second verse of that carol is 'I spied three ships come sailing by', and the fourth: 'And he did whistle, and she did sing, on Christmas Day in the morning.'

Sandys gave the carol a second wind and kept it in the water. He also printed it in the first person singular, bolstering a rare Christmas trend – the carol from 'my' perspective ('*I* saw three ships'). Not many carols are so personal, most others being descriptive and written in the third person or written in the first person plural ('we'). 'I sing of a maiden' is another example, whereas in 'Away in a manger' the meditative 'I' only comes in halfway through ('I love thee Lord Jesus'). Other 'cradle songs', tend to use 'we', the main exception being 'Cradle Song' by Isaac Watts (1674–1748).

The plot thickens when we consider the legend that underlies the maritime scenario. It is not about Mary and Bethlehem at all, but rather about the relics of the magi being transported to Cologne Cathedral. Behind the high altar is a sarcophagus containing the bones of three men of different ages. Opened and inspected in 1864, the shrine is the largest reliquary in the western world, built between 1180 and 1225. The story goes that Helena, mother of the Emperor Constantine (c. 272–337), found their bodies and took them to Constantinople, and later Eustorgius took them to Milan. In 1162 the skulls were sent to Cologne by the Holy Roman Emperor Fredrick Barbarossa. According to the *New Oxford Book of Carols* (1992), a version of 'I saw three ships' sung by Humber River boatmen contains the lines: 'I axed 'em what they'd got on board… They said they'd got three crawns… I axed 'em where they was taken to… They said they was ganging to Coln upon Rhine… I axed 'em where they came frae…. They said they came frae Bethlehem.'

Once we get Germanic, we find a 14th-century carol called 'Es kompt ein Schiff geladen', the first verse of which may be translated as:

> *There comes a ship that's laden*
> *and rich her precious hoard:*
> *God's son most gracious*
> *and his eternal word.*

It goes on to speak of a valuable cargo, of love as sails and the Holy Spirit as the mast. The ship drops anchor, and thus the Word made flesh comes into land. Jesus is born in a Bethlehem stable, and whoever would gladly kiss and adore him must endure his pains and anguish, must die with him, and rise to win that eternal life, which he alone brings about.

The idea that the Word made flesh arrives by boat is fanciful and delightful, but it also hints of an undercurrent of theological meaning. Mystically, we might think of Mary as the vessel in which salvation is borne to the world. Roman Catholic devotion still thinks of her in this way; Cardinal John Henry Newman (1801–90) described her as the 'vessel of honour'. We might also remember that many churches have a 'nave', a word which means 'ship', so in a sense we are all in the boat that navigates the seas of earthly life before we cross over to the shores of heaven.

Meanwhile, if we think less about the journey and the ships, and more about the mention of three of them, could it be that Father, Son and Holy Spirit come 'sailing in' on Christmas morning as the Trinity comes into full glory with the incarnation of God made human in Jesus Christ? Ships, sailors, donkeys, camels and magi aside, this carol helps us remember this if only by its threefold mention of the trinity of ships. Meanwhile, seafaring metaphors for faith abound, and however we find or interpret them, the idea of having Jesus on board through the storms of life is a comforting and inspiring one (see Luke 8:22–25). For we are all on board those three ships of faith, hope and love.

God who is three in one and one in three, until the day when we reach the shore, guide us and guard us as we sail in hope, assured of the promises revealed in the birth, death and resurrection of Jesus Christ our Lord. Amen.

13 NO CRYING HE MAKES

Away in a manger

Away in a manger, no crib for a bed,
the little Lord Jesus laid down his sweet head;
the stars in the bright sky looked down where he lay,
the little Lord Jesus asleep on the hay.

The cattle are lowing, the baby awakes,
but little Lord Jesus no crying he makes.
I love thee, Lord Jesus, look down from the sky,
and stay by my side until morning is nigh.

Be near me, Lord Jesus; I ask thee to stay
close by me forever, and love me, I pray.
Bless all the dear children in thy tender care,
and fit us for heaven, to live with thee there.

Words: Authors uncertain; vv. 1–2: *Little Pilgrim Songs* (1883); v. 3: *Gabriel's Vineyard Songs* (1892).
Music: 'Cradle song', William J. Kirkpatrick (1838–1921)

This most beloved of Christmas cradle songs, vital for all crib services, first appeared in *Little children's book: for schools and families. By authority of the general council of the Evangelical Lutheran Church in North America*, published in Philadelphia in 1885. Some people believe that Martin Luther wrote it because James R. Murray printed the text with his own tune, 'Mueller', in *Dainty Songs for Little Lads and Lasses*, published in Cincinnati in 1887, and called it 'Luther's Cradle Hymn (composed by Martin Luther and still sung by German mothers to their little ones)'. Given the dating of the text, this cannot be true.

The third verse was not included by Murray because it had not been written, only being traceable to a volume edited by the Lutheran pastor and gospel song composer Charles Hutchinson Gabriel, entitled *Gabriel's Vineyard Songs*, published in Louisville in 1892. According to Bishop William F. Anderson, it was written by John Thomas McFarland sometime between 1904 and 1908, but this also cannot be true. Most hymn books avoid confusion by attributing anonymity to the whole text, veiling its complex provenance.

The differing origin and style of the third verse annoys some hymnological purists. Hymns are invariably addressed to God or Christ or to ourselves, and rarely does a hymn change direction midway. 'Away in a manger' begins by describing Jesus asleep and not crying and then in the final two lines of what is now the central verse, the singer changes direction and addresses the baby Christ: 'I love thee…' The third verse continues in that vein, with a touching prayer, as by a child, for all other children.

The whole text does not bear theological or scriptural scrutiny, and to pay it such attention is to miss its point and purpose. The notion that the baby Jesus did not cry flies in the face of the fundamental humanity to which God incarnate must surely be attributed. Babies cry; they just do. If they never do, there is likely to be something seriously wrong. We do not need to think of Jesus as a non-crying baby; indeed it helps us to appreciate his humanity, fragility and vulnerability if we think of him as doing so. If on the other hand we see the phrase 'no crying he makes' as a momentary one, such that he is content and asleep, then the lovely image of a sleeping baby is evoked and that seems entirely normal. It is not that he never cries, only that he is not crying now.

Here is the Christ-child, from a child's point of view, presented *for* children, to be worshipped *by* children. No wonder every children's carol service has to use it, and it is one of the few songs that children still learn by heart before they can read. It is perhaps the first experience of worship that many children have, and one of the few utterly unifying songs that children now sing, in school or church. That parents and grandparents learnt it too gives the cradle song a golden thread of faith and joy that stretches beyond its relatively brief history.

To sing this carol is to become a child again. In one sense we do not follow Paul, who says: 'When I was a child, I spoke like a child, I thought like a child, I reasoned like a child. When I became an adult, I put an end to childish ways' (1 Corinthians 13:11). Rather we are reminded: 'Beloved, we are God's children now' (1 John 3:2). As God's children we sing this cradle song to the fragile human being who is God incarnate. He is not crying, but one day his sweat will fall like blood and our tears will flow for recognition of our sin as he dies on the cross.

There are at least 41 tunes for 'Away in a manger!' Three are reasonably well-known, one of which is a traditional tune from Normandy – a beautiful setting, sometimes sung by the choir at a carol service. To British singers, there really is only one tune, and being ubiquitous at school and church nativity services, many people can sing 'Away in a manger' without any text or music being provided. 'Cradle song' is by

William J. Kirkpatrick, a keen musician and composer from Pennsylvania, who wrote many hymn tunes and led worship from the violin or 'cello. It was first heard in the musical *Around the World with Christmas* in 1895.

In the United States another tune is preferred, Murray's 'Mueller'. It is possible to sing 'Mueller' and 'Cradle song' at the same time, in harmony, something I realised when in Bethlehem, at the supposed site of the birth of Jesus underneath the Church of the Nativity. Groups from all over the world visit, and it seems essential for pilgrimage groups to sing 'Away in a manger' in that holy place. To do so one must queue, sometimes for hours, and the sound of 'Cradle song' or 'Mueller' rise from the shrine below successively, or even simultaneously!

Wherever we are from and whichever tune we sing, we are singing the same hymn, and the worldwide nature of our faith can accommodate this diversity, which serves to unite us with Christians worldwide, singing the same hymn in a different way. That the two tunes work together says something profound about the depth and breadth of the gift of faith in the babe of Bethlehem, asleep on the manger hay.

Be near us Lord Jesus, and give us a childlike faith that offers love and commitment in the face of the cynicism and scepticism of our age. Hear our prayer for all your dear children, that they may sleep safe and secure, and keep us pure in body and mind, that at the last we may come to dwell with you and the Father, in the power of the Spirit. Amen.

SLEEP IN
HEAVENLY PEACE

Silent night

Silent night! Holy night!
All is calm, all is bright
'round yon virgin mother
   and child,
holy infant so tender and mild,
sleep in heavenly peace,
sleep in heavenly peace.

Silent night! Holy night!
Shepherds quake at the sight;
glories stream from heaven afar,
heav'nly hosts sing Alleluia:
Christ the Saviour is born,
Christ the Saviour is born.

Silent night! Holy night!
Comes salvation from the height,
down from heaven's shining scorn,
golden grace in human form,
God incarnate is born,
God incarnate is born.

Silent night! Holy night!
Where today power and might,
Father's love is now outpoured,
as a brother comes our Lord,
Christ to the people of earth,
Christ to the people of earth.

Silent night! Holy night!
Now the time comes aright,
as our God from sin us spares,
in himself atonement bears
that all the world be saved,
that all the world be saved.

Silent night! Holy night!
Son of God, love's pure light
radiant beams from thy holy face
with the dawn of redeeming grace,
Jesus, Lord, at thy birth,
Jesus, Lord, at thy birth.

Words: Joseph Mohr (1792–1848); vv. 1, 2, 6 translated by John Freeman Young (1820–85); vv. 3–5: translated by Gordon Giles (b. 1966)

Music: 'Stille nacht', Franz Xaver Gruber (1787–1863)

'Stille nacht' was written in 1818, and a century later it was being sung on both sides of the World War I trenches. Another century on and it is a global hit, one of the world's most popular carols, translated into many languages and performed in varying styles and genres. It was first sung by Franz Gruber and Joseph Mohr, the schoolmaster and parish priest of the little Austrian parish of Oberndorf, not far from Salzburg.

Some of the further information that is often quoted or repeated at Christmas about this Austrian cradle song is pure fiction. The legend has it that Father Mohr wrote the carol when the church organ was damaged by mice and could not be fixed (a different version of this is that the river flooded and broke the organ). Faced with no music for midnight Mass, he hastily wrote a song and presented it to his organist. Gruber was impressed and set the words to a lullaby which was sung that evening, accompanied on the guitar. However, the broken organ is an American invention from the 1930s, and the Christmas Eve performance in 1818 was well-planned. Mohr had written the words in 1816, when he was parish priest in Mariapfarr, 90 miles away. He had moved parishes for the sake of his health. The pair sang it as a duet, with the latter playing the guitar. The choir had practised singing the last two lines of each verse as a refrain. Authentic performances of the original version of 'Stille nacht' are enlightening in this respect: the carol is very different now to what it was, although it is still very recognisable.

Mohr had had a musical education under Michael Haydn, the younger brother of the more famous Joseph Haydn. His mother was abandoned by his father, a soldier, so he was adopted by the clergy of St Peter's Church, Salzburg, where he was trained to sing in the choir. Ordination followed, and Mohr gained a reputation as a down-to-earth priest, who sang bawdy songs, drank with men and flirted with women. Nevertheless he remained a parish priest until his death in St Johann in 1848.

His text is far more reverent: from the original German, of which there are many divergent translations, Mohr's verses are often mixed up, such that a three-verse version uses lines from all six verses. In his original text, verse 1 is all about the holy 'pair' (Mary and Joseph) looking on their curly haired sleeping baby boy. Verse 2 describes how when the holy child laughs with the mouth of God, we are struck with the realisation that this is the hour of salvation. Verse 3 speaks of God's salvation poured down in human form from the golden height of heaven.

There are three further verses, the fourth of which tells how the power of God's fatherly love makes Christ embrace all the peoples of the world as brothers, and verse 5 carries us to creation, at which point God, angry at sin, plans salvation for the world. Mohr's final verse moves to the shepherds in the field, who are the first to hear the angels' 'Alleluia'. The central verses are rarely sung, and not in English. I have created what I hope is a useable form above, in keeping with the theology and text of Mohr's text. Using them might enable something of authentic length and content to be sung in English to either the original version of the tune or the smoother modern one.

The history of 'Silent night', like the history of any significant cultural or religious object, is the history of humanity. What we have done to and with a hymn or song says as much about us as it does about the song itself. Looking back over the past two centuries we notice that halfway between now and then, this gentle Christmas hymn was wafting across the pockmarked chasms of the trenches, inviting shell-shocked troops to lay down their arms for a day or two and engage in the marginally more friendly activity of an Anglo-German football match. Its creators could never have imagined or foreseen that, although they might have been pleased. It was a unique moment in the history of war and peace. Yet soon the *himmlisches ruh* – the heavenly peace that had descended – lifted, and the cacophony of horror and slaughter continued unabated until the war finally ended.

There is some irony in the fact that Oberndorf is not far from the Kehlsteinhaus ('Eagle's Nest'), the retreat for Hitler built in the mountains above Berchtesgaden. Although the original church in Oberndorf was demolished after floods in 1905, the popularity of the carol led to a Silent Night Chapel being built as a tourist attraction. A day trip to that region could easily include both places, one extolling the virtues of heavenly peace as declared by the angels, and the other representing the dark and brutal history of the Third Reich. Such contrasts pervade modern life: we sing romantic carols about a baby boy born at Bethlehem, while remembering the trials and tribulations that that little town has suffered over two millennia of sin and strife.

We love the 19th-century idea of Christmas, with yule logs and music boxes that play 'Silent night', yet also try to worship the Christ-child in the manger as the harbinger of something uniquely profound and significant. The history of a carol informs its meaning, and its use colours our opinion of it. However saccharine – or bitter – we might find its multilayered modern context to be, we should not lose sight of its meaning and purpose, which is still true at Christmas or at any time. Just as the angels sing of peace on earth, we pray fervently for peace on earth in our time. For Christmas, with its bittersweet notes, is at root a time to celebrate the birth of, and worship, the Prince of Peace.

Jesus, you are the perfect Christmas gift, who first came to us in the silence of a holy night. As 'the dawn of redeeming grace', fill your world and our hearts with compassion and heavenly peace, here, and now, and in every place. Amen.

15 CHRIST, BY HIGHEST HEAVEN ADORED

Hark! the herald angels sing

Hark! the herald
angels sing,
Glory to the newborn king;
peace on earth and mercy mild,
God and sinners reconciled.
Joyful all ye nations rise,
join the triumph of the skies;
with the angelic host proclaim,
Christ is born in Bethlehem.

Hark! the herald angels sing,
Glory to the newborn king.

Christ, by highest heaven adored,
Christ, the everlasting Lord;
late in time behold him come,
offspring of a virgin's womb!
Veiled in flesh the Godhead see,
hail the incarnate Deity!
Pleased as man with man to dwell,
Jesus, our Emmanuel.

Hail the heaven-born
   Prince of Peace!
Hail the Sun of Righteousness!
Light and life to all he brings,
risen with healing in his wings;
mild he lays his glory by,
born that man no more may die:
born to raise the sons of earth;
born to give them second birth.

Come, desire of nations, come,
fix in us thy humble home;
rise, the woman's conquering seed,
bruise in us the serpent's head.

Now display thy saving power,
ruin'd nature now restore;
now in mystic union join
thine to ours, and ours to thine.

Adam's likeness, Lord, efface,
stamp thy image in its place;
second Adam from above,
reinstate us in thy love.

Let us thee, though lost, regain,
thee, the life, the inner man;
O, to all thyself impart,
form'd in each believing heart.

Words: Charles Wesley (1707–88), George Whitefield (1714–70), Martin Madan (1726–90), Charles Burney (1726–1814) and William Hayman Cummings (1831–1915)
Music: 'Mendelssohn' (also known as 'Berlin' or 'St Vincent') from a chorus by Felix Mendelssohn-Bartholdy (1809–47), adapted by William Hayman Cummings

The Christmas hymn we now know as 'Hark! the herald angels sing' did not start out life as such, and at least four people have brought it to its current and fixed form. Now glued in place at Christmas Eve and Christmas Day services, as well as carol services and concerts, the version we know and love was already so fixed by 1904 that when the editors of *Hymns Ancient and Modern Revised* tried to reinstate Wesley's original words, there was a national outcry and both *The Daily Mail* and *The Daily Express* condemned them, proposing that the hymn book should be withdrawn. The latter even accused them of perverting Wesley's original words, which they were attempting to restore!

The texts are similar, but there are some noticeable differences. Wesley's original, written as a Christmas Day hymn in 1738 (the year of his conversion) and first published in 1739, is made up of ten four-line verses, rather than the longer eight-line verses with refrain to which we have become accustomed. It was probably the organist and composer Charles Burney who adapted the hymn to three eight-line verses and his version appeared in 1769, published in Martin Madan's *Lock Collection*. Madan also made a few textual amendments.

Wesley's original began with:

> *Hark, how all the welkin rings,*
> *'Glory to the king of kings;*
> *peace on earth, and mercy mild,*
> *God and sinners reconcil'd!'*

'Welkin' is an Old English word, used by Chaucer, Shakespeare and Wordsworth, which means 'sky' or 'vault of heaven'. In this original version of Wesley's, the heavens ring with the phrase 'Glory to the king of kings', echoing Luke's 'Glory to God in the highest heaven' (Luke 2:14). George Whitefield, who had been a student with Wesley, altered this in 1753, maintaining the four-line verses but changing the angels' emphasis: 'Glory to the newborn king' means something slightly, but significantly, different.

A careful look at the gospel account reveals that the angels praise *God*, whereas in 'Hark! the herald angels sing', they are described as praising *Jesus*, which is slightly different, inaccurate biblically and rarely noticed. Furthermore, Luke does not write that the angels 'sing', but rather that they praise God '*saying*' (Luke 2:13), so it may well be that this reinterpretation by Whitefield has helped cement the popular notion of angels singing the 'Gloria'.

At the time Wesley refused to sing Whitefield's reworking of his words, furious that he had presumed to alter them to suit his own ends. Whitefield also omitted the final verses, and the loss of them is a genuine theological one. The seventh verse quotes the Advent antiphon 'Come, desire of nations, come', followed by a reference to the fall, with the serpent bruising the heel of humanity and Adam bruising its head (Genesis 3:15). Wesley cleverly alters the meaning, asking that the serpent in us (sin) should be bruised (defeated) by Christ, the second Adam, who reinstates us as beloved children of God. In the restoration of sinful humanity to a state of grace through the incarnation of Christ, the joining of divine and human nature is also achieved. Consequently, that which was lost (salvation) is gained and a new life is granted to all believers.

The tune used then has been forgotten, swept away by the popularity of the tune with which the German composer Felix Mendelssohn is credited and which bears his name. It comes from the second chorus of his 'Festgesang an die Kunstler' ('Festival song for an artist') – 'Gott ist Licht' ('God is light'). It was William Cummings, organist of Waltham Abbey, who adapted the melody in 1855. The work was written for and first performed in Leipzig in June 1840 at a festival commemorating the 400th anniversary of the achievements of the inventor of printing, Johannes Gutenberg (1400–68). The text was as follows:

Vaterland, in deinen Gauen
brach der goldne Tag einst an.
Deutschland, deine Völker sahn
seinen Schimmer niedertauen.
Gutenberg, der deutsche Mann,
zündete die Fackel an.

Which translated means something like:

Fatherland, in your country
the golden day once dawned.
Germany, your people saw
its shimmering decline.
Gutenberg the German man,
lit the glorious torch.

While we may not want to celebrate Gutenberg in this way nowadays, the 'Gutenberg Bible' was the first of many editions of the greatest book in history, in which is contained the account of the Word made flesh and the story of Christ in words. So perhaps it is fitting that such a great Christmas hymn should have its musical beginnings in a piece praising the man who did so much to make the mass distribution of the Bible possible for future generations.

Mendelssohn himself said that his tune should not be set to sacred words, declaring that it was too militaristic. Similarly, Wesley, when writing the original text, suggested that a slow, solemn tune would fit them best. Just as with the hymn 'Dear Lord and Father of mankind', neither the composer nor the lyricist consented to or ever heard the marriage that was made of their creative endeavours.

Nevertheless, 'Hark! the herald angels sing' has become part of the institution of Christmas, sung in churches and streets. It also sounds out some wonderful theology, reminding us that Jesus, the newborn king, is Prince of Peace, Sun of Righteousness, everlasting Lord, incarnate Deity and Emmanuel, 'God with us'. It endures not only as a vehicle for mass praise, but also as a reminder of the great gift that our Father God has given us in his Son Jesus Christ, and which we celebrate not only at Christmas but any day.

Glory to you O Christ, our newborn king! By the light and life which you bring, reconciling sinners, come and dwell in our hearts, so that we too may join the triumph of the skies, where in highest heaven you are adored by saints and angels singing your praises, now and always. Amen.

16 BE BORN IN US TODAY

O little town of Bethlehem

O little town of Bethlehem,
   how still we see thee lie!
Above thy deep and dreamless sleep
   the silent stars go by.
Yet in thy dark streets shineth
   the everlasting light;
the hopes and fears of all the years
   are met in thee tonight.

O morning stars, together
   proclaim the holy birth,
and praises sing to God the king,
   and peace to men on earth.
For Christ is born of Mary,
   and gathered all above,
while mortals sleep the angels keep
   their watch of wondering love.

How silently, how silently,
    the wondrous gift is given;
so God imparts to human hearts
    the blessings of his heaven.
No ear may hear his coming,
    but in this world of sin,
where meek souls will receive
    him still,
        the dear Christ enters in.

Where children pure and happy
    pray to the blessed child,
where misery cries out to thee,
    son of the mother mild;
where Charity stands watching
    and Faith holds wide the door,
the dark night wakes, the
    glory breaks,
        and Christmas comes once more.

O holy child of Bethlehem,
    descend to us, we pray!
Cast out our sin and enter in,
    be born in us today.
We hear the Christmas angels,
    the great glad tidings tell;
O come to us, abide with us,
    our Lord Emmanuel!

Words: Phillips Brooks (1835–93)
Music: 'Forest Green', Ralph Vaughan Williams
(1872–1958)

The writer of the hymn about the little town of Bethlehem, Phillips Brooks, was an American bishop. By all accounts he was universally respected and loved, and he preached the sermon when Abraham Lincoln's body lay in state in Pennsylvania in April 1865. Eight months later, on 30 December 1865, he was visiting the Holy Land and wrote these words to his father:

> After an early dinner [we] took our horses and rode to Bethlehem. It was only about two hours when we came to the town, situated on an eastern ridge of a range of hills, surrounded by its terraced gardens. It is a good-looking town, better built than any other we have seen in Palestine. The great Church of the Nativity is its most prominent object; it is shared by the Greeks, Latins and Armenians, and each church has a convent attached to it. We were hospitably received in the Greek convent, and furnished with a room. Before dark, we rode out of town to the field where they say the shepherds saw the star. It is a fenced piece of ground with a cave in it (all the Holy Places are caves here), in which, strangely enough, they put the shepherds. The story is absurd, but somewhere in those fields we rode through the shepherds must have been, and in the same fields the story of Ruth and Boaz must belong. As we passed, the shepherds were still 'keeping watch over their flocks,' or leading them home to fold. We returned to the convent and waited for the service, which began about ten o'clock and lasted until three (Christmas). We went to bed very tired.

Three years after visiting the little town, Brooks wrote 'O little town of Bethlehem'. He had in mind the prophecy in Micah:

> But you, O Bethlehem of Ephrathah,
>> who are one of the little clans of Judah,
> from you shall come forth for me
>> one who is to rule in Israel,
> whose origin is from of old,
>> from ancient days.
>
> MICAH 5:2

Unlike many writers of 19th-century Christmas carols, Brooks had actually been to Bethlehem. Many imagine it to be an idyllic and peaceful place; modern times would not paint it so. While the angels over Bethlehem sang of peace, we have struggled with it ever since. Peace has become the great hope of Christmas, yet year by year Christmas preachers rattle off a catalogue of places where there is not peace on earth. One of those places where, if there is peace, it is very fragile, is Bethlehem itself. Located six miles from Jerusalem, in the Occupied Palestinian Territories of the central West Bank, it is a draw for tourists and pilgrims, mostly for the Church of the Nativity and the outlying Shepherds' Field.

The idea that Bethlehem is a place where new beginnings might be hoped for is poignant when we recall that Jesus was born in an oft-besieged little town. Weaving Christmas past with Christmas present, we hold in tension the joy to the world that God's gift of Jesus is to us, but also lamenting the very present reality that the peace and goodwill which the angels proclaimed is a Christmas present from on high that is still yet to be unwrapped in the very place where it was first delivered.

Brooks was alert to the gap between hope and reality, which was as wide then as now, in the Holy Land, in the USA and in Victorian Britain. The oft-omitted fourth verse speaks of the contrast of hope and despair, and calls to us to work and pray for a better world. The birth of the Christ-child is not wholly about a holy baby who makes no crying, born in a stable under miraculous circumstances, with a mission to fulfil and a world to save. Of course, on one level it is, but that is done, that is in the past. We do not look to the past in hope; we look to the future, and our hopes for the future are located not in the past, but in the present.

'Emmanuel' means 'God with us', not 'God *was* with us two millennia ago'. If we say that, we are saying that God has been and gone. God is not gone. God – Emmanuel – is with us, and so our prayer, borrowed from the exquisite last verse of the hymn is: 'Be born in us today.' Whatever the little town of Bethlehem was, and is, and even what it will become, in any event, we locate the incarnation of God, the coming of our Saviour, to the here and now, and in you and me.

Christmas is about the first coming of Jesus, born over 2,000 years ago. The second coming is what we focus on in Advent – the time when Christ shall return and the world will end. There is another coming, the one that really matters, the one that is personal, the one that gives us true hope, peace and joy – that is the coming of Christ to each and every one of us, the birth of the Saviour in our own hearts. It can happen any day. On each and every day, we can pray, with Phillips Brooks, that the little town of Bethlehem be not far away, but in our very beings.

Bethlehem is in us, and it is the place from where we call Christ to come to us, to abide with us and to truly be our Lord Emmanuel, God with and in us.

God of past, present and future, by your Spirit, make your dwelling in us this Christmas, that the message of peace and hope which was born in Bethlehem may radiate from our lives and inspire action which casts out sin and brings hope to a dark world. Amen.

MOST HIGHLY
FAVOURED LADY

The angel Gabriel from heaven came

The angel Gabriel from heaven came,
   his wings as drifted snow, his eyes as flame.
'All hail,' said he, 'thou lowly maiden Mary,
most highly favoured lady!' Gloria!

'For lo! a blessed mother thou shalt be,
all generations laud and honour thee.
Thy Son shall be Emmanuel, by seers foretold,
most highly favoured lady!' Gloria!

Then gentle Mary meekly bowed her head.
'To me be as it pleaseth God,' she said;
'My soul shall laud and magnify his holy name.'
Most highly favoured lady! Gloria!

Of her, Emmanuel, the Christ, was born
in Bethlehem, all on a Christmas morn.
And Christian folk throughout the world will ever say,
'Most highly favoured lady!' Gloria!

Words: Sabine Baring-Gould (1834–1924)
Music: Basque traditional

By now we are clinging to Advent for dear life as we acknowledge that Christmas is effectively both now and not yet. There is a chink of light between the fourth Sunday of Advent and Christmas Eve. Sometimes it is the same day. As the hours count down to Christmas Day, we may try to live in that spiritual space, anticipating Christmas and joining in with all the mirth and light, while trying to continue to recognise the more sombre period of Advent with its weekly themes. These are the patriarchs, the prophets, John the Baptist and Mary.

The end of Advent brings us through biblical history to the point where Mary, the unknown girl from Galilee, is suddenly given the great commission to be the mother of Jesus, the Son of God. It is the culmination of Advent and the beginning of Christmas. It is the pivot of spiritual, global history. So there is a sense of Advent *and* Christmas as a sort of either/or that is also a both/and. Rather like the annunciation.

The annunciation is so much part of our western culture, an event which has captured imaginations and inspired art and music, sculpture and even architecture. Wonderful as it all is, it is difficult to unwrap the covering it comes in, difficult to access the core of the story, tricky to examine, investigate, question or indeed understand it. It is a paradox – the impossible event that so many want to believe in, the crucial happening that sets western thought, culture and faith in motion.

To negotiate the annunciation, we need to think in two modes, for it is a very human story *and* an other-worldly one. It introduces the dual nature of Jesus Christ as divine and human, and it is the foundation of the idea of Mary as *Theotokos* – God-bearer. Her child, the angel Gabriel tells her and us, is also God: two-in-one, inseparable, both/and not either/or.

Thus this dual-being baby needs to be handled in a dual-mode way, rather like saying it is both Advent *and* Christmas. It cannot be both, of course. But, of course, it *is*. We have to speak in two languages at once. We have been doing so since the beginning of December. We speak the language of Advent, which is all about waiting for the return of our Lord and judgement, light and darkness, penitence and anticipation. Meanwhile the language of Christmas cannot wait, is brightly lit with multicoloured decorations, merriment and gratification. They are almost the opposite, in fact, yet simultaneous: both/and. One of these languages could be English; the other Latin.

This is something we find in the Basque carol which narrates the annunciation – 'The angel Gabriel from heaven came'. Entitled 'Birjina gaztettobat zegoen', it was 'discovered' by the Revd Sabine Baring-Gould (he of 'Onward, Christian soldiers' fame) around 1907. As a young boy he had spent a few months in the Basque region, which straddles France and Spain and which at various times in history has sought independence from both nations. Baring-Gould, the son of an Indian calvary officer, became rector of Lew Trenchard in Devon in 1881, where he and his Yorkshire-born wife settled. They had 15 children, but he also found time to study the folksongs of the south-west of England, to translate hymns from Scandinavian languages and to write a novel and the multi-volume *Lives of the Saints*. I spotted a full set on sale in a second-hand bookshop recently.

His Basque-based carol was first published in 1922, but it was not until 1971 that the words and music as we know them were published together and became widely used. The text is in two languages – Latin and English – the languages of Advent and Christmas if you will. It is macaronic in that it has verses in English and a refrain, 'Gloria', in Latin. As we have seen already, 'Ding dong, merrily on high!' does a similar thing, as does 'Angels from the realms of glory'. These languages can coexist in the carol, just as, analogously, the languages of Advent and the language of Christmas can.

At this time of year the church needs to speak both languages as part of a mission to everyone during this sombre, joyous month of December. We must not neglect Advent, but nor can we bang on about 'it not being Christmas yet'. People do not want to hear that. People do not *understand* that. For just as many people do not speak Latin these days, increasingly they do not speak the language of Advent, rather assuming and expecting all the Advent stuff can be translated into Christmas-ish. But this means that much is lost in translations and that half of the voices – the Advent voices – are not heard.

There are different voices in Advent stories, and we need to pay attention to them all. We need to hear the angel, and we need to listen to Mary. Gabriel's is a divine voice – the voice of an angel, a messenger. Mary's is a woman's voice. There are no men speaking in the story of the annunciation. In fact, there are no men speaking in Advent overall. Zechariah, John the Baptist's father, is the main man until the annunciation, but he is struck mute – silenced. Zechariah cannot speak, and Joseph does not speak. It is Mary and Elizabeth who speak, and we hear their emotions as well as their words. Advent is a time to listen to the women. For the sound of Advent is the voice of women, and the silence of Advent is the silence of men.

If we listen to Mary's voice, and Joseph's silence, what do we hear? Can we hear what they hear? As Advent draws to a close and Christmas rushes in, let our silent prayers and voiced praises be according to God's word, who as Word made flesh, *borne by* Mary and *born of* Mary, comes to dwell in our hearts once again and always.

Heavenly Father, as you sent an angel to Mary bearing good news for all people, enlighten and enrich us with the good news of your love for us all. And, as we are reminded of the birth of your Son Jesus Christ, come and dwell in our hearts, that we too may leap to your voice and live our lives in the steady rhythm of mercy on which our faith is founded. This we ask through the same Jesus Christ our Saviour. Amen.

18 GOOD TIDINGS WE BRING

We wish you a merry Christmas

We wish you a merry
Christmas,
we wish you a merry Christmas,
we wish you a merry Christmas
and a happy New Year.

Good tidings we bring
to you and your kin.
We wish you a merry Christmas
and a happy New Year!

We wish you a merry Christmas…

Now bring us some figgy pudding,
now bring us some figgy pudding,
now bring us some figgy pudding,
now bring some out here.

Good tidings we bring…

We wish you a merry Christmas…

For we all like figgy pudding,
for we all like figgy pudding,
for we all like figgy pudding,
so bring some out here.

Good tidings we bring…

We wish you a merry Christmas…

And we won't go till we've got some,
and we won't go till we've got some,
and we won't go till we've got some,
so bring some out here.

Good tidings we bring…

We wish you a merry Christmas…

Words and music: Traditional, arranged by Arthur Warrell (1883–1939)

The first recorded use of the phrase 'Merry Christmas' is often claimed to have been by John Fisher, the bishop of Rochester, on 22 December 1534. It occurs in a letter, written from his imprisonment in the Tower of London, to Thomas Cromwell, chancellor to Henry VIII. He complains of being cold and hungry, saying his clothes are 'ragged and rent', and revealing that he can only eat certain meats, otherwise he gets coughs and diseases. He begs for release from prison and concludes:

Other twain things I must also desire upon you: that one is that it may please you to that I may take some priest within the Tower to hear my confession against this holy time; the other is, that I may borrow some books to stir my devotion more effectually these holy days for the comfort of my soul. This I beseech you to grant me of your charity. And thus our Lord send you a merry Christmas and a comfortable to your hearts desire.

At the Tower, the 22nd day of December.

Your poor Beadman,

JO. ROFFS.

A 'beadman' is one who prays for someone else, so, even in confinement and discomfort, he prays for those who might well be considered his enemies and wishes them well. John Fisher had been a tutor to King Henry, yet, along with Thomas More, he lost his life for disagreeing over the 'great matter' of Henry's second marriage to Anne Boleyn.

As well as offering prayers, Fisher wishes those who have imprisoned him a 'merry' Christmas. In 1520, 14 years earlier, Charles Booth, the bishop of Hereford from 1516 to 1535, wrote to one of the canons of the cathedral: 'I pray God you may be in all good charity and merry this Christmas.' The phrase is not quite the same, but the intention is similar and the circumstances more cheerful.

'Merry' is an old English word, used by Chaucer, for example, in the Clerk's Prologue of *The Canterbury Tales*. It is derived from the Old English *myrige*, which was more akin to pleasant or agreeable rather than joyous or jolly. The feast of the nativity of Jesus has been celebrated since at least the fourth century, and the word 'Christmas' has been used since at least the eleventh century. Its meaning is straightforward: the Mass – or Eucharist – of the birth of Christ. Nevertheless, the word does not actually contain any direct reference to the *birth* of Jesus.

That it took 400 years to join these words together into a greeting seems strange. Neither Fisher nor Booth should be credited with 'inventing' the conjunction nor using it for the first time. They did not use it in their letters in an identical manner and both were likely following an evolving seasonal convention. 'Merry Christmas and a happy new year' adds another dimension and is first traced to an informal letter written in 1699 by Admiral Frances Hosier to Robert Smith, a storekeeper at the Deptford dockyards in London.

In *A Christmas Carol* (1843), Charles Dickens' Ebenezer Scrooge objected to the word 'merry', saying: 'If I could work my will… every idiot who goes about with 'merry Christmas' on his lips should be boiled with his own pudding.' Nevertheless he changes his tone after the visit from the ghosts of Christmas past, present and future: 'I am as merry as a school-boy. A merry Christmas to everybody!'

'Merry Christmas' has become a daily December greeting, resounding nicely with 'and a happy new year'. The carol which uses this phrase as its mainstay has helped cement it in the English-speaking psyche. It is perhaps surprising therefore to note that it does not even date from the Victorian era, but rather from the 20th century. Although sometimes claimed to be a Tudor song from Somerset, collections of folk songs from that region do not include it, nor even does the *Oxford Book of Carols* (1928). It may be tempting to date it to around the time of Bishop John Fisher, but there is little evidence for that.

We know the song thanks to Arthur Warrell, and it was likely first performed by the University of Bristol Madrigal Singers on 6 December 1935. Warrell was assistant organist at Bristol Cathedral and then became organist at Clifton Parish Church as well as a lecturer in music at the University of Bristol. Some have suggested that he actually wrote 'We wish you a merry Christmas', which found its way into the first volume of *Carols for Choirs* (1961) and has since become an encore at carol concerts and services. While it is widely believed that this is an old carol with a modern harmonisation that can be taxing for choral singers, its bursting into 20th-century Christmas culture as both a choral item and a carol singers' doorstepping song may be more or less simultaneous.

This ubiquitous Christmas song therefore has little known history and even less spiritual significance. Indeed its text might even be interpreted as being greedy and pushy. Singers demand a sweet treat and refuse to leave until it is forthcoming! Jolly and 'merry' as it might seem, Christmas is about gift, not payment or extortion. Salvation is God's gift, offered – and sometimes rejected – in the fragile babe of Bethlehem, who in unassuming, rough but righteous manner, takes on human flesh and is born among us, unnoticed in a borrowed room.

Nowadays, amid the revelry and the Christmas songs which do not mention the birth of Christ and which focus on jollity and an enthusiasm for indulgence and escapism, the silent voice of salvation is often crowded out as the language of merriment prevails. Figgy pudding is sweeter than bitter herbs, and giving carol singers treats and some money is easier than struggling with the plight of the people and places where peace and justice are in short supply.

For there is always a bitter taste to our merriment, however we mask it. Bishop John Fisher was only wishing Thomas Cromwell and Henry VIII a 'merry Christmas' because he was locked in the Tower of London, cold and hungry. The dark world of Dickens' London is illuminated by Scrooge's conversion to generosity, yet we might well remember that there are still many who are cold and hungry today and others who are persecuted for their faith or beliefs. The Universal Declaration of Human Rights of 1948 promulgated freedoms of thought, conscience and religion, the forbidding of torture and slavery, entitlements to law and justice, education and health and wellbeing. We are not there yet.

Jesus, at this merry time of year, when bright lights, songs and delicious smells fill the air, keep us mindful of those who are hungry and cold, who thirst for righteousness and justice and endure the harsh realities of suffering, conflict or deprivation. May they find inner merriment in the comfort and joy provided by those who love them in your name. Amen.

19

WHEN WE WERE GONE ASTRAY

God rest you merry, gentlemen

God rest you merry, gentlemen,
let nothing you dismay;
for Jesus Christ, our Saviour,
was born upon this day,
to save us all from Satan's power
when we were gone astray.

    O tidings of comfort and joy.

From God, our heav'nly Father,
the blessed angel came,
and unto certain shepherds
brought tidings of the same:
how that in Bethlehem was born
the son of God by name.

    O tidings of comfort and joy.

The shepherds at those tidings
rejoicéd much in mind,
and left their flocks a-feeding
in tempest, storm and wind,
and went to Bethlehem straightway
this blessed babe to find.

   O tidings of comfort and joy.

But when to Bethlehem they came
whereat this infant lay,
they found him in a manger,
where oxen feed on hay;
his mother Mary kneeling
unto the Lord did pray.

   O tidings of comfort and joy.

Now to the Lord, sing praises
all you within this place,
and with true love and brotherhood
each other now embrace;
this holy tide of Christmas
all others doth deface.

   O tidings of comfort and joy.

Words: Traditional, anonymous, *Roxburgh Ballads* (c. 1770), William Sandys' *Christmas Carols, Ancient and Modern* (1833)

Music: John Playford's *The English Dancing Master* (1651); Edward Francis Rimbault's *A Little Book of Christmas Carols* (1846), arranged by John Stainer, *Christmas Carols New and Old* (1871)

While 'We wish you a merry Christmas' has little theological or biblical content and cannot be traced much further back than the 20th century, this much older carol, while also anonymous, has a greater heritage and a more 'Christian' feel to it, being found in hymn books and carol sheets alike. It is also associated with door-to-door carol singing.

In the British Isles there are so many regional traditions and approaches to singing at Christmas time that it is a complex business to unravel and articulate them all. Some of these traditions are allegedly medieval in origin and are connected to singing in pubs and the west galleries of churches, sometimes to the annoyance of the vicar. Some of our well-known scriptural carols, such as 'While shepherds watched their flocks by night', were sung in this way, and consequently they have many tunes associated with them.

The culture of Christmas was strong within the hearts of men and women, who enjoyed singing and sharing the gospel narrative and conveying good cheer, goodwill and the good news. Carols were the songs of the people, and they did with them what they liked and where they liked. Sometimes the gospel narrative took a back seat, and as carol singing took to the streets, we might trace a development from 'While shepherds watched', which is purely biblical, via 'God rest you merry, gentlemen' to 'We wish you a merry Christmas'. Some of these songs may be described as 'luck-visit' songs, carols sung when visiting a house in expectation of food and drink. The phrase 'rest you merry' can be traced to Sir Thomas Elyot's 1548 *Dictionary*, in which he writes: 'As the vulgare people saie, Reste you mery.' To my mind this settles the debate as to where the comma goes in the text – between 'merry' and 'gentlemen'; the phrase was in common use.

'Cheers,' they said and sang as some warming drink was given and received. We still do it and from it we get the notion of 'Christmas cheer', which invariably involves eating and drinking. Thus the narrative falls away, even if the goodwill and good cheer remain. This is to some extent what has happened to Christmas, as western culture defaces the season, removing the baby Jesus in whose holy face we see all humankind. Christmas has moved from annunciation to consumption, and our carols both reflect and contribute to this direction of travel.

Charles Dickens knew 'God rest you merry, gentlemen', and in *A Christmas Carol* Ebenezer Scrooge, hearing it sung through the door of his office, 'seized the ruler with such energy of action, that the singer fled in terror'. Eleven years later, Dickens' *The Seven Poor Travellers* (1854) describes a group of carol-singers performing on a winter's evening: 'I heard the Waits at a distance, and struck off to find them. They were playing near one of the old gates of the City.'

Street carol-singers remain and, bearing appropriate licences and collection buckets, still wander the streets and gather in corners of pubs, railway stations and super-markets. I spend a fair amount of time as we approach Christmas with my flute, playing carols with singers in various places, raising money for charity. Buskers sing all year round, usually collecting money for themselves. Carol-singing has become a charitable activity, and much money is raised by singing Christmas hymns and carols and rattling a tin or brandishing a new-fangled 'touch and pay' device so that commuters can donate as they pass by. Children stop to dance, and tourists video the whole thing and post it on social media: this quaint tradition of singing in public places at Christmas. (I tried Easter and then Harvest hymn-singing at a local station one year, which was fun, and arguably 'missional', but raised hardly any money, provoking bemusement rather than generosity!)

Carol-singing is thus a weird and wonderful tradition only possible in December. It blends together so many of the individual strands that accompany the season: gospel, goodwill, generosity, proclamation, food, wine and jollity. That many carols have their origins in dance tunes and rhythms adds a dimension of movement, still found in street – and church – processions while singing. Try singing 'God rest you merry, gentlemen' as a processional hymn in church and a certain sway, inherent in the 6/8 (compound) metre of the tune, will creep into and be transmitted through the feet!

The direction of travel between the street and the church goes both ways. While we might speak of singing in two languages at Christmas, we also travel in two directions, and 'God rest you merry, gentlemen' is an example of a carol that has found its way into liturgical use. Our Christmas carols take us from church to porch, and vice versa. There is a verse, absent from hymn books and not sung in churches, which is homely:

God bless the master of this house,
And misteress also,
God bless the little children
All around the table go,
God bless the friends and kindreds
That come both far and near.
May the Lord send a happy new year.

Even the version used ecclesiastically has 'Now to the Lord sing praises, all you within this place', which can refer to the church as easily as anywhere else, but it reveals the roving origin of the carol. Singing it in the street carries it back to its origins as a form of itinerant street preaching! For it proclaims the saving birth of Jesus, the fall and redemption, the wonder of the shepherds, Mary and the manger. Then it moves into a greeting and a blessing of the occupants of the house and final exhortation to give each other a hug. In this sense it is a both/and carol, not an either/or, for the gospel remains at its heart and bids us embrace each other and our Lord.

Jesus, may we embrace you and your saving grace this Christmas. As we sing of your incarnation in streets and churches at this time, break through the cheery mists of goodwill and feed us with true love that we may bring your comfort and joy to all people at this holy tide of Christmas. Amen.

20 THE LOVE SONG WHICH THEY BRING

It came upon the midnight clear

It came upon the midnight clear,
   that glorious song of old,
from angels bending near the earth
   to touch their harps of gold:
'Peace on the earth, good will to men
   from heaven's all-gracious king.'
The world in solemn stillness lay
   to hear the angels sing.

Still through the cloven skies
   they come
   with peaceful wings unfurled,
and still their heavenly music floats
   o'er all the weary world;
above its sad and lowly plains
   they bend on hovering wing,
and ever o'er its Babel-sounds
   the blessed angels sing.

But with the woes of sin and strife
   the world has suffered long;
beneath the angel-strain have rolled
   two thousand years of wrong;
and man, at war with man, hears not
   the love song which they bring.
O hush the noise, ye men of strife,
   and hear the angels sing!

And ye, beneath life's crushing load,
   whose forms are bending low,
who toil along the climbing way
   with painful steps and slow,
look now! for glad and golden hours
   come swiftly on the wing.
O rest beside the weary road
   and hear the angels sing!

For lo! the days are hastening on
   by prophet bards foretold,
when, with the ever-circling years,
   shall come the age of gold;
when peace shall over all the earth,
   its ancient splendours fling,
and the whole world give back
   the song,
   which now the angels sing.

Words: Edmund Hamilton Sears (1810–76)
Music: 'Noel', traditional, arranged by Arthur Sullivan
(1842–1900)

This hymn, often sung at Christmas midnight services, most likely because it contains the word 'midnight', does not explicitly mention the birth of Jesus. It is about angels, rather than Christmas, and in the *Revised English Hymnal* (2023) it is found not in the Christmas section, but in the collection of hymns assigned to Michaelmas (29 September). The hymn's author, Edmund Sears, was a Massachusetts Unitarian minister who claimed to be descended from one of the original pilgrim fathers who set sail on the Mayflower in 1620. Unitarians do not generally believe in the divinity of Jesus Christ, preferring to see him as an ethically righteous, divinely inspired saviour, who is not God incarnate nor a person of the holy Trinity.

Written and published in 1849, when Sears was minister at the First Church in Wayland, Massachusetts, the song dates from a time of illness and despair in his life and period of war in Europe, and between the United States and Mexico. It crossed the Atlantic in 1870 and was placed in the 'Church Triumphant' section of *The Hymnal Companion to the Book of Common Prayer*. Sears himself considered it to be a Christmas hymn, positioning it next to a Christmas Eve sermon in his *Sermons and Songs of the Christian Life* (1875). Yet because of its content, rather than the intentions associated with this hymn, some do not consider it to be a Christmas carol. However, as it does not express an authentic trinitarian expression of Christian incarnational theology, this might make it more singable by those who do not believe. In a world where many carols and hymns expressing a solid theology of Christmas are sung by those who do not believe a word of it, this song about peace and goodwill, heaven and hope, may be sung with a lesser need for integrity than some others.

The ethical and aspirational dimensions of the text are worthy and by no means incompatible with Christian ethics and beliefs. Phrases such as 'prophet bards' and 'age of gold' are not grounded in Christian culture and teaching, however, and some have criticised the text for their use. It is not entirely clear what Sears meant by them. They are probably not a reference to the American gold rush or to some future prophecy, although in some hymn books the hymn is headed by the line 'I heard the voice of many angels' from Revelation 5:11. The age of gold might be the end of the age, and the prophet bard the writer of Revelation.

There are many angels in the hymn, messengers of God and bringers of peace. As with some other Christmas hymns, the idea that the angels *sing* is assumed, while the idea they play the harp also comes from Revelation:

> And I heard a voice from heaven like the sound of many waters and like the sound of loud thunder; the voice I heard was like the sound of harpists playing on their harps.
> REVELATION 14:2

In Revelation 5:8 the elders hold harps, too, although there is no suggestion that the harps are golden. Nevertheless, the first verse of this carol is clearly referencing the angels in Luke 2, heralding the birth of Jesus to the shepherds. The second verse tells us that the song they sang then is still being sung: the message of peace which they brought to Bethlehem is still as valid, and necessary.

The reference to Babel (see Genesis 11:1–9) reminds us of the divisions amid humanity that the confusing multiplicity of languages represents. This idea of nations and people divided by language is also metaphorical, relating to religion, race, culture, colour, temperament. Yet we are united in the recognition of, and desire for, an end to division and enmity, which is actually what this poem is all about. For in the 2,000 years since the birth of Jesus, not much has changed: the clamour of war drowns out the song of peace.

The song could end there, without controversy. The fourth verse is often omitted, while the fifth verse has been edited at various times. Here are two examples:

O Prince of Peace, thou knowest well
this weary world below;
thou see-est how men climb the way
with painful steps and slow.

O still the jarring sounds of earth
that round the pathway ring,
and bid the toilers rest awhile,
to hear the angels sing.

Church Hymns, 1874

O Prince of Peace, on whom we cast
our every cross and care,
come enter thou our longing hearts,
and make thy dwelling there;
and may we 'mid our daily toil
to thee our praises bring,
until on high we learn the song
that now the angels sing.

The Westminster Carol Book, 1899

These attempts to Christianise or alleviate confusion or heresy have not taken hold, and most hymn-book editors have opted for Sears' original, without verse four. 'Giving back the song' which the angels have sung is a rather lovely idea which completes the circle, and the revised verses are not generally reckoned to better it.

The eminent Victorian composer Arthur Sullivan gave us the tune used in the UK, which he based on a traditional folk tune and called it 'Noel'. He preferred not to set Sears' last verse, not because of its theology but because it did not fit the metre of the tune. The emphasis on the word 'the' in 'And *the* whole world give back the song' is clumsy, and he preferred the version from *Church Hymns*, of which he was the editor. These words fit, but they are not as good. Perhaps the simple solution would be something like, 'And *all the world* give back the song, which now the angels sing.'

In any event, Christians, Unitarians and all the world can sing in sympathy with the sentiments of this spiritual song which extols the gift and need for peace in every age.

God, who in Jesus took upon yourself human nature as word incarnate, help us to believe what we sing and sing what we believe. Bring peace and harmony to your world, that the hope and faith you bring may sound in the love songs which we sing. Amen.

21 LORD OF ALL THIS REVELLING

What sweeter music

What sweeter music can we bring
than a carol, for to sing
the birth of this our heavenly king?
Awake the voice! Awake the string!
Heart, ear, and eye, and every thing
awake! the while the active finger
runs division with the singer.

[From the flourish they came to
     the song].

Dark and dull night, fly hence away,
and give the honour to this day,
that sees December turn'd to May.

If we may ask the reason, say:
the why, and wherefore all things here
seem like the spring-time of the year?

Why does the chilling winter's morn
smile, like a field beset with corn?
Or smell, like to a mead new-shorn,
thus, on the sudden?

Come and see
the cause, why things thus fragrant be:
'tis he is born, whose quick'ning birth
gives life and lustre, public mirth,
to heaven and the under-earth.

We see him come, and know him ours,
who, with his sun-shine, and his
     showers,
turns all the patient ground to flowers.

The darling of the world is come,
and fit it is, we find a room
to welcome him.

The nobler part
of all the house here, is the heart,

Which we will give him; and bequeath
this holly and this ivy wreath,
to do him honour; who's our king,
and Lord of all this revelling.

Words: Robert Herrick (1591–1674)
Music: John Rutter (b. 1945)

It would be very odd to write about Christmas carols in this day and age and overlook one of our most noted living composers, who has likely written more published Christmas music than any other composer. A carol service without something by Sir John Rutter is an unusual one, and examples such as the 'Candlelight Carol', the 'Star Carol', the 'Shepherd's Pipe Carol', the 'Nativity Carol' and many others delight singers and listeners alike. The catalogue is by no means closed: the recent 'Joseph's Carol' was written as a musical tribute to the Oxford scientists who worked on the Covid-19 vaccine in 2020. That carol, like so many, deployed lyrics he specially wrote.

'What sweeter music' is a little different, being a setting of words by the English poet Robert Herrick. He lived through the English Civil War, and as a Royalist supporter of King Charles I (who was beheaded in 1649), he became known as a 'Cavalier poet'. Herrick was also a clergyman, ordained in 1623, having studied at St John's and then Trinity Hall in Cambridge. This put paid to his apprenticeship as a goldsmith. In 1629 he became the vicar of Dean Prior in Devon. He was ejected from this living in 1647, only being allowed to return in 1662, after the restoration of the monarchy, remaining there until his death aged 83.

His Christmas poem was first published in *His Noble Numbers: or, His Pious Pieces* (1647) with six verses and three sections, which Herrick called 'choruses'. (Most carol settings do not use it all.) It was headed 'sung to the King in the presence at

White-Hall', which suggests it was composed some years before being published. It was largely forgotten until it reappeared in *The Illustrated London News* in 1845.

Eighteen years later, in an article published in *Once a Week*, an 'illustrated miscellany of Literature, Art, Science and Popular Information' (1863), Edmund Sedding commented: 'Some twenty or thirty years ago, we should scarcely have dared to predict the resuscitation of the Christmas carol.' His article began with the opening lines of Herrick's text, but he could have been speaking about the revival of carol-singing in general, which he claimed was 'little better than a respectable scheme for raising money'.

A musical setting finally appeared in 1928, in *The Oxford Book of Carols*, set by Martin Shaw to a tune which derived from a German nativity play. Since then, the carol has been set to music by several contemporary composers. Richard Rodney Bennett (1936–2012), Bob Chilcott (b. 1955) and Will Todd (b. 1970) have all done so, while Philip Stopford (b. 1977) is probably the most recent to do so. It is perhaps no surprise, because this is a carol about carol-singing and Christmas music.

Rutter's is perhaps the most famous, and his luscious tune and harmonies much-loved. Written in 1987 for Stephen Cleobury and the choir of King's College, Cambridge, it was first heard at the Festival of Nine Lessons and Carols traditionally broadcast on Christmas Eve. Rutter described it as:

The first opportunity I had to put pen to paper for the choir in my long and friendly association with King's College. I particularly enjoyed the opportunity to write for the slot in the service immediately after the reading about the journey of the Wise Men – the chance to highlight in the text the idea of the gifts that we can bring.

Rutter's association with King's College goes back to his days when, as an undergraduate at Clare College, he attended a harmony and counterpoint class taught by David Willcocks (1919–2015). He told the young John to show him some examples of his work. The rest is history: Willcocks was impressed with the 'Shepherd's Pipe Carol' (written when Rutter was 18), and his career began. Rutter says: 'It was thanks to his kindness that I first made the leap from being an aspiring composer to a published composer, and it would never have happened if I'd been assigned to a different harmony class.'

The text celebrates the birth of Christ. It draws out the darkness of the December Advent season, but likens the brightness of Christ's birth to the month of May. We wonder how and why the season seems like spring. The cause is the birth of Jesus, 'whose quickening birth give life and lustre'. The 'darling' is the child, whose coming to earth prompts us to find room, not so much in a cattle shed, but in the heart. The carol turns in the last lines, in which the sentiment is expressed that the holly and ivy and all the trappings of Christmas tradition, then and now perhaps, should be dedicated to this newborn King.

This simple thought and gesture is profound and helpful. Christmas is full of revelry and triviality, of baubles and bonhomie. Such activity can seem inappropriate to a celebration of incarnation, or it can get in the way of the true meaning of Christmas. Or it can be redirected, as Herrick proposes. For it is Christ who is 'Lord of all this revelling' and to him we can give the laurels of holly and ivy. It is the thought that counts. As we have seen in so many of our Christmas carols, they can operate on two levels or have a double meaning. A carol can be secular *and* sacred. Even the secular or pagan can become sacred if reassigned, directed heavenward. Any music becomes sweet if brought in praise, thanksgiving, wonder and homage.

For the object of our prayers and praises is the Lord God, the Holy One of Israel, who as a vulnerable child, took on human flesh and was born for us, to redeem us and bring us the hope of resurrection life, wrapped in love and received in faith. What sweeter music *can* we bring than a carol, for to sing (of) the birth of this our heavenly king? None surely.

*O holy child, whose arrival heralded a new age of grace
and peace, help us turn all our Christmas celebrations
towards you and the salvation you brought by your birth,
life, death and resurrection. Turn the poverty of our praise
into the sweet song of heavenly acclamation. Amen.*

22 FALL ON YOUR KNEES

O holy night

O holy night, the stars are brightly shining;
it is the night of the dear Saviour's birth.
Long lay the world in sin and error pining,
till he appeared and the soul felt its worth.
A thrill of hope the weary world rejoices,
for yonder breaks a new and glorious morn.
Fall on your knees, O hear the angel voices!
O night divine! O night when Christ was born.
O night, O holy night, O night divine!

Led by the light of faith serenely beaming,
with glowing hearts by his cradle we stand.
So, led by light of a star sweetly gleaming,
here come the wise men from Orient land.
The king of kings lay thus in lowly manger,
in all our trials born to be our friend.
He knows our need, to our weakness no stranger!
Behold your king! Before him lowly bend!
Behold your king, your king! Before him lowly bend!

Truly he taught us to love one another;
his law is love and his gospel is peace.
Chains shall he break, for the slave is our brother,
and in his name all oppression shall cease.
Sweet hymns of joy in grateful chorus raise we,
let all within us praise his holy name!
Christ is the Lord, then ever, ever praise we!
His pow'r and glory, evermore proclaim!
His pow'r and glory, evermore proclaim!

Words: Placide Cappeau (1808–77), translated by John Sullivan Dwight (1813–93)
Music: Adolphe Adam (1803–56)

This song frequently tops the Christmas carol charts and lays claim, in the UK at least, to be 'the nation's favourite carol', according to Classic FM, the 'home of Christmas music'. The popularity is surely based on a masterfully sublime tune, evocative words and sumptuous harmonies, which, spread out as arpeggios, create a serene depiction of a calm, starlit Christian scene.

It has traditionally been used to begin midnight Mass on Christmas Eve throughout the French-speaking world. The birth of Jesus is associated with midnight, because the shepherds are keeping watch over the flocks 'by night' (Luke 2:8) and we assume that the angels tell them immediately and that they then go straight to the manger nearby. Unlike some aspects of the nativity story that have been embellished, the idea that Jesus was, as the carol by Geoffrey Ainger puts it, 'born in the night' is scriptural. It is true literally and metaphorically, for, as Philips Brooks put it in another carol that speaks of a holy child born on a holy night, the everlasting light comes to dark streets.

The 'world in sin and error pining' can be interpreted as referring to wicked actions fuelled by greed, power, cruelty and hatred and founded on fear, frailty and foolishness. In the French original it is more explicitly original sin. Traceable back to Adam and Eve, it is the sin which none can cleanse, the state of fallen human nature which makes sinners of all, whatever we say or do. It is the kind of sin which can only be wiped away by the birth – and death – of a Saviour. There is atonement for original sin in the French, the dark side of Christmas, which we do not find in the lighter touch of the English-language version, which prefers a new and glorious dawn and angel voices instead.

In its original form, 'O holy night' gives us both a literal and a metaphorical midnight, a real and a spiritual darkness when Jesus was born into a world which contains not only people who commit sins, but a world in which each and every one of us is a sinner in need of redemption:

> *Minuit, chrétiens, (Midnight, Christians)*
> *cest l'heure solennelle (it is the solemn hour)*
> *ou l'Homme Dieu descendit jusqu'à nous (when the man-God descended to us)*
> *pour effacer la tache originelle (to wipe away original sin)*
> *et de Son Père arrêter le courroux. (and end his Father's anger)*

Here we see the wrath of God, angry at human sin. In the second verse, there is a similar toning down of the atonement dimension:

> *À votre orgueil, (To your pride)*
> *c;est de là que Dieu prêche (from which God preaches)*
> *courbez vos fronts (bow your foreheads down)*
> *devant le Rédempteur. (before the Redeemer)*

The English translation of this song softens its text and calms the scene, no more than alluding to the depths of inner spiritual darkness which beset the world and to which the author was making reference, even though he professed to be an atheist.

Born in Roquemaure near Avignon, Placide Cappeau had to have a hand amputated after another child shot him with a gun with which he was playing. This prevented him following his father's profession as a barrel-maker and he took up drawing, educated at the expense of the father of the boy who had injured him. He studied literature and law, but became a wine merchant, dealing with barrels, rather than making them. A local priest asked Cappeau to write a song to raise funds, and he wrote the text on 3 December 1843 (some say 1844) in the carriage on the way to Paris, somewhere between Mâcon and Dijon. When he arrived he tracked down the famous and popular composer Adolphe Adam, who agreed to set the words, and their 'Cantique de Nöel' was first performed on Christmas Eve 1844, back in Roquemaure. Unsurprisingly it was a great success, even though it was written by someone who did not believe in God or original sin and did not like clergy much.

John Dwight, like Edmund Sears, who wrote 'It came upon the midnight clear', was a Unitarian from Massachusetts. He founded a musical journal in 1852 and specialised in the music of Bach and Handel. In 1855 he translated Cappeau's words, softening the theology, as we have seen. For some, Dwight's version resonates with his abolitionist views ('Chains shall he break, for the slave is our brother'), while for others it has the distinction of being the first piece of music ever played on a radio. On 24 December 1906, the Canadian inventor Reginald Fessenden broadcast on AM for the first time and, after reading from the opening of Luke's gospel, played 'O holy night' on the violin.

We should not let the carol's distinctive history and somewhat unusual provenance cloud what the text invites us to *do*. No other carol instructs us so directly to 'fall on your knees' ('*Peuple a genoux, attends ta délivrance!* '), to bow your faces to the ground ('*Courbez vos fronts*'). We hear of shepherds, magi, even animals kneeling before the Christ-child, and we picture them doing so as St Francis did at Greccio in 1523 or as in Thomas Hardy's poem of 1915, 'The Oxen': 'Christmas Eve, and twelve of the clock. "Now they are all on their knees."' Yet Cappeau and Dwight entreat *us* to kneel in worship. We are not to observe a tableau, but rather to participate in it, to join in, to get involved and make the worship our own.

Christmas is not a spectacle; midnight Mass is not a show. Theatrical as some liturgy may seem, perhaps loaded with luscious music, processions, incense and evocative lighting, the worship is immersive. It is a cold heart that observes the drama dispassionately or fails to be transported to that musical place where mystery is manifestly real and the heart is warmed by the Spirit of God who helps us pray, even when we do not know how to pray as we ought, interceding with sighs too deep for words (see Romans 8:26). For then, even the prayers of non-believers may rise to the heavenly throne of God. Here is hope for those without hope, for those who do not know what hope is. 'For in hope we were saved' (Romans 8:24), and we kneel patiently in adoration amid the silence and the sounds of a holy night.

Bring us to our knees, O God, that we, like the magi, may join in worship of the divine Christ-child. With countless generations and saints and angels in heaven, may we glorify you and hail the dawn of the new day of redemption, hope and love, revealed in the birth of the same Jesus Christ our Lord. Amen.

23 YEA, LORD WE GREET THEE

O come, all ye faithful

O come, all ye faithful, joyful and triumphant,
O come ye, O come ye to Bethlehem;
come, and behold him, born the king of angels.

O come, let us adore him,
O come, let us adore him,
O come, let us adore him,
Christ the Lord.

God of God, light of light,
Lo! he abhors not the virgin's womb;
very God, begotten not created.

See how the shepherds, summoned to his cradle,
leaving their flocks, draw nigh with lowly fear;
we too will thither bend our joyful footsteps.

Lo! star-led chieftains, magi, Christ adoring,
offer him incense, gold and myrrh;
we to the Christ-child bring our hearts' oblations.

Child, for us sinners poor and in the manger,
fain we embrace thee, with awe and love;
who would not love thee, loving us so dearly?

Sing, choirs of angels, sing in exultation,
sing, all ye citizens of heaven above;
glory to God, glory in the highest.

Yea, Lord, we greet thee, born this happy morning;
Jesus, to thee be glory given;
Word of the Father, now in flesh appearing.

Words: John Francis Wade (1711–86), translated by Frederick Oakeley (1802–80), William Thomas Brooke
(1848–1917) and William Mercer (1811–73)
Music: 'Adeste Fideles', 18th-century melody, attributed to John Wade, descant by David Willcocks
(1919–2015)

'O come, all ye faithful' is a hymn, and it finds its rightful place as such at Christmas services on Christmas Eve and Christmas Day on which it would be almost unthinkable not to sing it. The final verse, beginning 'Yea, Lord we greet thee, born this happy morning…', is a very special Christmas Day or midnight Mass moment, and many will not sing it at any other time. Doing so preserves that spine-tingling moment in the middle of the night when the faithful who have come to church can sing and feel that Christmas has truly arrived.

So many Christmas hymns and carols have been purloined for commercial use and have been filling the airwaves for the preceding month that when 'Yea, Lord we greet thee' strikes up, with its extravagant harmonies, it is almost as if Christmas is there reclaimed for its proper purpose. The final verse is the culmination of Advent, and those who observe Advent in the face of the 'run-up to Christmas' save a special chamber in their hearts for this musical acclamation of the completion of one season and the commencement of another. It is therefore a special and moving musical movement to sing 'Yea, Lord we greet thee, born this happy morning' at the right time and not a month, week, day or hour before. To some extent this distinguishes the faithful from the folkful.

Broadly speaking, the hymn traces the gospel Christmas story, from virgin birth to the magi's visit. Written originally in Latin, each verse describes from an observer's point of view how the shepherds, angels, magi and then we ourselves come to worship – to adore the newborn king. We join with them in space and time to acclaim Christ as Lord. As pilgrims to the manger ourselves, we are observers and participants in the nativity scene. Yet what distinguishes this Christmas hymn from many carols is the attitude of *worship* we adopt. 'O come, all ye faithful' is a joyful and triumphant call to worship, not simply a retelling of the events of Christmas.

The text and tune first appeared in England in 1782, and it was sung in 1795 at the chapel of the Portuguese embassy, a safe haven for Catholic worship. The Duke of Leeds referred to it as 'the Portuguese hymn', causing a great deal of subsequent confusion. It may be because it was written by Portuguese friars of the observance of the Order of St Peter of Alcantara (known as Arabadoes), who came to England in 1667, when invited by Catherine of Braganza (Charles II's wife) to live in and serve the Chapel Royal. They served the court of Charles II and then King James II and his wife, Mary of Modena, from 1685.

At the Queen's Chapel at St James' Palace, a carol service for the royal household is still held, at which they sing the Latin version:

Adeste Fideles laeti triumphantes,
Venite, venite in Bethlehem.
Natum videte, Regem Angelorum;
Venite adoremus,
venite adoremus,
venite adoremus
Dominum!

A carol in Latin was never going to become popular in reformed, Anglican Britain. In 1841, however, the same year that Prince Albert introduced the nation to Christmas trees, Frederick Oakeley, an incumbent of Margaret Street Chapel, London (now All Saints', Margaret Street), translated it into English for use there. The opening line was 'Ye faithful, approach ye', but in 1845 he rewrote it as: 'O come, all ye faithful, joyfully triumphant.' The fourth and fifth verses of 'Adeste Fideles' were not translated by Oakeley, but by William Mercer, an Anglican priest.

Until very recently the main tune was thought to have been written by John Francis Wade, who is also supposed to have written the original Latin words. He was an English Roman Catholic who became involved in the Jacobite rebellion in Scotland and was a supplier of music to expatriate Roman Catholics. This may explain why this relatively modern hymn was written originally in Latin, which in the mid-18th century was still very much the language of the Roman Catholic Church. It was published in Wade's *Cantus Diversi* in 1751, probably having been written around 1740.

Another special and popular aspect of the hymn is the descant by Sir David Willcocks to which it is wedded. Anecdotally he once remarked that he would sometimes go to churches in his native Cornwall where he would find that not only the choir, but the congregation were singing his ubiquitous descant. He also suggested that perhaps eventually the descant would in fact become the tune, rather as had happened with 'The first Nowell'. Willcocks died in September 2015, after a distinguished and illustrious career as organist, choral director, composer and arranger of music, especially carols. The *Carols for Choirs* series was shaped by him, firstly with Reginald Jacques and then John Rutter. The series is fundamentally a Cambridge phenomenon, being originally the songbook of the King's College Nine Lessons and Carols from King's services, and it is still a major force in the continuing development of Christmas carols worldwide. Willcocks deserves most of the credit for this burgeoning interest in Christmas hymns and carols since the 1970s.

Lord Jesus, as we follow the light of your star to Bethlehem, to greet your appearing and hail your presence among us, grant us, your faithful people, so to adore and follow you, not only on this day, but all the days of our lives, until we come to dwell with you and sing your praise with choirs of angels and all the citizens of heaven. Amen.

24 ON THE BUMPY ROAD!

The Camel Carol

We sing our song, we camels three,
of gold and myrrh and frankincense.
We tread the sand, O tired are we:
we've got the hump today!
Three magi proudly sitting on high
on the bumpy road!

With wise a sage sat on my back,
incense for faith I bring to the king.
A smelly weight, the load I pack
is on my hump today.
Through wind and heat and scorching sun,
on the bumpy road!

I bear the gold: a wealthy hope
for all the world, a promise unfurled.
These riches for a newborn babe
are on my hump today.
He comes to us from God most high
on the bumpy road!

With myrrh on my mound I look around
at all the love we offer the king.
A perfumed jar the magi found
is on my hump today.
Crossing now the vale of death
on the bumpy road!

So join our song as now we sing
on bumpy way to Bethlehem,
with faith and hope and love to bring
on our humps today.
Three graces: gifts on our camels' backs
on the bumpy road,
on the bumpy road!

Words: Gordon Giles (b. 1966) © 2023 Stainer and Bell, used with permission
Music: Thomas Hewitt Jones (b. 1984)

As this book nears its conclusion, I hope the reader will permit me a little self-indulgence as we turn to a recently composed carol, the words of which I wrote in summer 2023. I first met Thomas Hewitt Jones when he played the organ at one of the Christmas services that take place in Rochester Cathedral during the Christmas Dickens Festival. Soon afterwards I sat down on a train and found him sitting opposite me in the carriage.

It was not such a long journey from the high-speed train from London to the camel train we find in this carol. Hewitt Jones is a former organ scholar of Gonville and Caius College, Cambridge, and he won the BBC Young Composer of the Year competition in 2003. As well has having a significant musical pedigree (with musical parents and grandparents), he has also written the ubiquitous 'Funny Song', which has had billions of online streams worldwide. It is the combination of modern popular savvy and classical underpinning that enables him to write for both genres and mingle them. 'The Camel Carol' is a blend of modern Christmas carol writing, for choirs to enjoy singing in a way that is neither too easy nor too difficult, but which also has a text that, even though it has a quirky feel, has strong theological resonances.

I came up with the idea of focusing the 'story' on the camels. There are many carols about the manger, the angels, the shepherds, the donkeys, oxen and asses, and of course the magi (or kings as many insist on calling them; there is only one king in the Christmas story – Jesus, the king of kings!) Hymns and carols that focus on the magi emphasise them and their gifts. Traditionally gold is for kingship, frankincense for worship and myrrh to prefigure the sacrificial death to which Jesus will submit. These are traditional and well-established interpretations and meanings, and they are embedded in this carol too.

Yet in a similar way in which 'The little road to Bethlehem' and 'Little donkey' focus on the animal, I wanted to present the birth of Jesus from the perspective of three camels who must trudge across the desert bearing the eastern sages and their precious presents. Camels are notoriously temperamental, so I imagined them as grumpy beasts of burden, 'getting the hump' on the bumpy road to Bethlehem. For in that region it is likely they would have had one hump each, not two.

The three gifts are not in the traditional order, because I have also associated them with the three Christian graces of faith, hope and love, found in 1 Corinthians 13:13. In the third century the theologian Origen figured that, because there were three gifts, there must have been three gift-givers, and these have been translated into kings because of a reference in Psalm 72 that refers to kings from Saba bearing gifts. Yet in the Bible the gifts are brought by an unspecified number of magi. Three is an important number in Christianity, signifying the Trinity. Faith, hope and love, which the apostle Paul has handed on to us as emblems for discipleship, are great virtues, and by God's grace, love is the greatest.

Furthermore, the Christmas story is grounded in faith, hope and love: faith in God; hope in resurrection life; and the greatest love, shown by God for us in Jesus, who shows his love for us on the cross. It therefore seemed fitting that, as the three gifts prefigure the meaningful life, mournful mystery and loving mercy of Christ, these graces can also be attached to the three gifts. Thus we have incense for faith, gold for hope and myrrh for love.

There are other resonances too. The perfumed jar of myrrh is a reference to the woman who anoints Jesus' head with 'very costly ointment' (which might have been myrrh), which Jesus says was to prepare him for burial (Matthew 26:6–13). In some traditions, the woman is erroneously identified as Mary Magdalene, whose saintly symbol is a jar of ointment. In the carol that jar is connected to the magi who also bring a jar of myrrh to symbolise the inevitable passion of Christ. Thus the myrrh carries us into the valley of death found in Psalm 23: 'Though I walk through the valley of the shadow of death, I will fear no evil: for thou art with me; thy rod and thy staff they comfort me. Thou preparest a table before me in the presence of mine enemies: thou anointest my head with oil; my cup runneth over' (Psalm 23:4–5, KJV). Here is more anointing, so in this psalm we notice another connection with the myrrh-giving magi that is often overlooked.

The way the composer has set this line emphasises the dark, deadly meaning – and danger – of their journey across the rough, sandy desert to pay homage to the newborn king of kings. A long pause is reached, during which the singers and listeners are musically delayed in the valley of death. Nevertheless, as they reach 'death', the camels themselves find faith, hope and love in their mission and the final verse carries us all to a joyful conclusion as the bumpy road becomes a causeway of achievement, and the camels arrive to join in the celebrations.

The rhythmical lilt of the carol conveys the awkwardness of the journey. We felt that a time signature of seven beats in a bar creates an unevenness, a 'three-plus-four' lilt. It bears us forward, but it is edgy, risky, uneven. We hope that this conveys the bumpy terrain and the reluctant gait of the camels.

In this carol, we are the camels and they are us. We sing their song, but their initial begrudging reluctance to serve and ultimate recognition of salvation which comes through submission to a divine summons, can be our journey too. Who has not complained en route? Who has not endured hardship or found the weight of the call a little too heavy? The road of faith is a bumpy one, but we walk it in hope, assured by faith of God's unfailing love on the journey, through the valley of death, into resurrection light.

God, guide and sustain us on the bumpy road
of life. May our faith be strong, our hope secure
and our love for you unwavering. Amen.

25 NEED THEY NO CREATED LIGHT

As with gladness men of old

As with gladness men of old
did the guiding star behold,
as with joy they hailed its light,
leading onward, beaming bright,
so, most gracious God, may we
evermore be led to thee.

As with joyful steps they sped,
to that lowly manger-bed,
there to bend the knee before
him whom heaven and earth adore,
so may we with willing feet
ever seek thy mercy seat.

As they offered gifts most rare
at that manger rude and bare,
so may we with holy joy,
pure, and free from sin's alloy,
all our costliest treasures bring,
Christ, to thee our heavenly king.

Holy Jesu, every day
keep us in the narrow way;
and, when earthly things are past,
bring our ransomed souls at last
where they need no star to guide,
where no clouds thy glory hide.

In the heavenly country bright
need they no created light;
thou its light, its joy, its crown,
thou its sun which goes not down:
there for ever may we sing
Alleluias to our king.

Words: William Chatterton Dix (1837–98)
Music: 'Dix' from a chorale by Conrad Kocher
(1786–1872), adapted by W.H. Monk (1823–89)

We end with an Epiphany hymn, which is not really a Christmas carol. However, it is often used at Christmas carol services, such as the Festival of Nine Lessons and Carols, with which so many churches and cathedrals mark the days running up to Christmas. People like to attend carol services before Christmas rather than afterwards, even though, liturgically speaking, the Christmas season begins at the midnight service and evolves into the Epiphany season on 6 January. Strictly speaking the Christmas season can legitimately be considered to extend until Candlemas on

2 February. Try telling that to shopkeepers, schoolteachers, workplaces and social clubs! So clergy have to like it or lump it, and not get the hump on the bumpy Advent road that leads to Christmas Day!

'As with gladness' has a devotional scheme which brings the magical presence of the wise men into focus and helps us to emulate their journey of hope and faith. Each of the first three verses relates in four lines something of the historical event of the wise men journeying from the east, but then the latter two lines assist personal devotion. The format is similar to the classical form of the kind of prayer used formally in church – a collect; that is, as such-and-such has happened, so may we emulate it and be changed spiritually. In this way, statement of fact leads to article of faith and profession of desire or intention.

Yet Dix does not continue the hymn in this vein. The text is directed to Christ, and the final two verses are more directly prayerful, without the 'as–so' structure. Instead, the focus turns to heaven and eternity, the ultimate destination and finding-place for all who seek Christ in any age. In this hymn therefore, we have a twofold purpose: to relate the story of the magi and their journey; and to encourage us to see Christ as the light of the world, who though born in a humble manger becomes the one through whom redemption comes to all nations.

Dix was born in Bristol, attended Bristol Grammar School and worked for an insurance company in Glasgow. He did not enjoy good health, and it was during a period of illness that he produced some of his earliest and best hymns. 'As with gladness men of old' is said to have been written on 6 January 1858, although some say it was a year later. Either way, Dix wrote it on his sick bed, meditating upon the Epiphany gospel passage, Matthew 2:1–12. It was an instant success: in 1859 it was selected for a pilot edition of *Hymns Ancient and Modern*, and it appeared as one of the most modern entries in the full publication of 1861.

At the time Dix was criticised for his slightly sentimental and biblically inaccurate text, such that for the 1875 edition of *Ancient and Modern* he was forced to allow a couple of small revisions. In the second verse, 'He whom' became 'Thee whom', and 'manger-bed' was altered to 'lowly bed'. In the second line of the third verse, 'At thy manger' became 'At thy cradle' – despite traditional crib-scene piety, Matthew's gospel indicates that the magi visited the holy family in a house, not a stable:

> On entering the house, they saw the child with Mary his mother; and they knelt down and paid him homage. Then, opening their treasure chests, they offered him gifts of gold, frankincense, and myrrh.
> MATTHEW 2:11

Such criticism also condemns much great art depicting the magi worshipping the Christ-child in the manger! On the other hand, it hardly matters, claimed Dix, who clearly resented having to make his text biblically if not politically correct. More recent revisions have tried to make the hymn politically correct by making the opening line more inclusive, begging the question not so much as to whether the 'men of old' are people in general, but whether they may not actually have all been male, as some have recently suggested. Other attempts have been made to remove the antiquated use of the word 'rude', which in modern usage means something more unpleasant than 'uncultivated' or 'simple', which is what Dix evidently meant, underlining the inherent humility of Christ's nativity.

It is easy to be sidetracked by these concerns, which obscure the bigger picture of Epiphany, which, with or without the manger, is arguably an even more significant festival than Christmas. In many parts of the world, 6 January is celebrated as Christmas Day. As Western Christians pack up their Christmas trees and decorations, the Greek Orthodox world and Catholic Spain are giving presents and celebrating with the magi. There is surely no better time to exchange gifts than on the day when the magi brought Jesus their famous offerings of gold, frankincense and myrrh, symbolising kingship, worship and sacrifice. In this much, the gifts they brought emphasise Jesus' immense significance for the world as king, God and suffering servant.

So, as we have journeyed through the 'festive season', hopefully we have not been too sidetracked by baubles and mince pies, but can strive, like the magi, to seek out and pay homage to the Christ-child, our redeemer, guide and king.

Christ the morning star, illuminate our paths so that in seeking you we may be rewarded by your kingly presence, revealed first at Bethlehem and still made real by your Spirit in the world today. As many have with gladness found and followed your light over the years, lead us forward to our ultimate, heavenly destination, where you await us with mercy and joy. Amen.

26 EPILOGUE: ON THE FEAST OF STEPHEN

I t is said: 'Time and tide wait for no one.' We find an older version of the phrase in Geoffrey Chaucer's Clerk's Tale in *The Canterbury Tales*, which dates from about 1395: 'For though we sleep, or wake, or roam, or ride, ever flees the time; it will wait for no-one.' It is likely older, traceable at least to the previous century. Chaucer's phrase is not a maritime one, although it has been adopted in common usage, because tides, while not governed by time, do mark it out with some regularity. For many the phase is about ageing: time (tide) does not wait for anyone; we cannot control it or ignore it. A tide is not a set of waves upon the seashore, but rather an old reference to time and the seasons.

Nevertheless, the notion of Christmastide seems to work either way. Or it seems that as soon as we reach Christmas on 25 December, the tide of Christmas goes out very fast. During the month of December, its waves lap on the Advent shores, becoming increasingly strong until the week before Christmas when we are awash with carols, tree lights and seasonal adverts. Just as the leftovers are soon consumed or thrown away, so too is the idea of a Christmastide. The baby Jesus is thrown away like bathwater, while only a few cling on to the incarnation as a seasonal theme.

The liturgical Christmastide, which lasts at least for the twelve days of Christmas to Epiphany, is soon forgotten as New Year's Eve and Day approach. The proverb is reversed: 'No one waits for time nor tide'! The tide of Christmas ebbs out very fast, leaving a shore strewn with discarded wrapping paper and full dustbins. The decorations may remain for a week or so.

Some carols speak of Christmas 'tidings', greetings befitting Christmastide. In 'God rest you merry, gentlemen', we sing 'O tidings of comfort and joy', and we find an explicit reference to 'This holy tide of Christmas' in the final verse. Christmastide *follows* Christmas; it does not *precede* it. Yet as every year goes by it seems clearer that the secularisation of the festival has put Christmas at the end of the season, not the beginning. 'Christmas' begins on 1 December and concludes on Boxing Day. The first martyr, St Stephen, only gets a mention if 'Good King Wenceslas' is still being sung. The irony is that Wenceslas himself was also a Christian martyr, whose brutal end, like Stephen's, casts a poignant shadow over the celebrations. Rightly so, for the birth of Jesus is not just about birth, but about the cross and resurrection and all who lived and died proclaiming the truth of the incarnation, on which it is all founded and where it all began. It began in humility, and it ended in humiliation.

APPENDIX

I THE STORY OF GLORY

Told in words from Christmas carols

Long time ago in Bethlehem, when the snow lay round about, born for us on earth below, the dear Christ enters in.

Joseph was an old man; the angel Gabriel from heaven came, a gentle message bare he, deep in awe the maiden bowed to hear him say, 'Ave Maria, most highly favoured lady! He abhors not the virgin's womb: a blessed mother thou shalt be, all generations laud and honour thee.'

'Tell out, my soul, the greatness of the Lord!'

As Joseph was a walking: 'Little donkey, carry Mary', on the little road to Bethlehem. The stars in the bright sky, high above the Milky Way, may rock the king of heaven: we will rock you, rock you, rock you, when he comes to reign, the babe, the son of Mary.

Away in a manger, in the bleak midwinter, Mary bore Jesus, who died for us all. A stable place sufficed, where a mother laid her baby, born to raise the sons of earth, the prince of glory is his name. Glory to the newborn king, sapphire-paved courts for stable floor, who was rich beyond all splendour, rules the world with truth and grace.

While shepherds watched their flocks by night, past three a clock, on a cold winter's night that was so deep, they quake at the sight. Angels from the realms of glory came upon the midnight clear: cherubim and seraphim thronged the air – a heavenly vision appeared, verily the sky is riven with angels singing the first nowell: 'All glory be to God on high, peace on earth and mercy mild.' God's highest glory was their anthem still, as out of darkness we have light which made the angels sing. While mortals sleep, the angels keep their watch of wondering love.

The world in solemn stillness lay to hear the angels sing. The shepherds at those tidings, rejoiced in heart and mind. Summoned to his cradle, leaving their flocks, led by the light of faith serenely beaming, with glowing hearts: 'What is that light so brilliant, breaking here in the night across our eyes?'

Hail, thou ever blessed morn. O how blest that wondrous birthday! The Lamb of God appears promised from eternal years, Jesus, our Emmanuel. While fields and floods, rocks, hills and plains repeat the sounding joy, the great God of heaven is come down to earth: love came down at Christmas. Emmanuel within us dwelling, be born in us today.

The Word of the Father, now in flesh appearing, became incarnate and assumed this mortal body, when from sin to set us free, to save us all from Satan's power: he is God and Lord of all. The Ancient of Days is an hour or two old. Yet this young child, mild he lays his glory by, little Lord Jesus, no crying he makes, yet tears and smiles like us he knew. God with us is now residing. Heaven cannot hold him, light and life to all he brings, the hopes and fears of all the years begin and never cease.

This did Herod sore affray and grievously bewilder, in his raging, all young children to slay.

As with gladness, three kings from Persian lands afar, bearing gifts. Then entered in those wise men three, full reverently upon their knee, magi, Christ adoring, offered gifts most rare: gold of obedience, incense of lowliness and myrrh from the forest breathes a life of gathering gloom.

Now to the Lord, sing praises all you within this place, for unto us a boy is born, and he is Christ the Lord.

We wish you a merry Christmas…

APPENDIX

II LINKS TO VIDEOS OF THE HYMNS

1	Gaudete!	youtube.com/watch?v=bTbq2pPLW6I
2	Hymn to the virgin	youtube.com/watch?v=BQsv5W4KXpM
3	Past three a clock	youtube.com/watch?v=-tVkwBGEFt8
4	Ding dong, merrily on high!	youtube.com/watch?v=sHyGer5ELAQ
5	Joy to the world!	youtube.com/watch?v=KIMz95x2Zsk
6	Of the Father's heart begotten	youtube.com/watch?v=Pt75zI4kz6g
7	In the bleak midwinter	
	Holst	youtube.com/watch?v=xAzQIS4-MpY
	Darke	youtube.com/watch?v=yb9tHjuy9Hw

8	Once in royal David's city	youtube.com/watch?v=TT3cfXd3Shk
9	A great and mighty wonder *in German*	youtube.com/watch?v=bt4ZbIuobMg youtube.com/watch?v=M1aG8fhb8DY
10	The first Nowell	youtube.com/watch?v=MiuHJORnbKI
11	Angels from the realms of glory *'Iris'* *'Regent Square'*	youtube.com/watch?v=PrLoWt2tfqg youtube.com/watch?v=MQHKpSyWN78
12	I saw three ships *Cornish*	youtube.com/watch?v=9CkrL8f06xQ youtube.com/watch?v=y7TChVp09tc
13	Away in a manger *'Cradle song'* *'Normandy'* *'Mueller'*	youtube.com/watch?v=LgYU_3TnsaI youtube.com/watch?v=HeEV7snVO8Q youtube.com/watch?v=KtZ6rmdfUv8
14	Silent night *Original version*	youtube.com/watch?v=a9S9rHVjG-k youtube.com/watch?v=t_nYQzY9Ans
15	Hark! the herald angels sing	pbs.org/wgbh/christmas-tabernacle-choir/concert-2019/hark-the-herald-angels-sing/#:~:text=Felix%20Mendelssohn%20originally%20wrote%20the,suited%20to%20a%20sacred%20text
16	O little town of Bethlehem	youtube.com/watch?v=xjCyxe-ZZH0

17	The angel Gabriel from heaven came	**youtube.com/watch?v=L-Rv-J46gvM**
18	We wish you a merry Christmas	**youtube.com/watch?v=mtYhr4VDmOo**
19	God rest you merry, gentlemen	**youtube.com/watch?v=38AvzEuTv7I**
20	It came upon the midnight clear	**youtube.com/watch?v=jjvLBEk1UfU**
21	What sweeter music	**youtube.com/watch?v=3h-u6HYKe8I**
22	O holy night	
	Three verses	**youtube.com/watch?v=SqIjlIjt-nI**
	Two verses	**youtube.com/watch?v=Y1oLk54R5Xg**
23	O come, all ye faithful	**youtube.com/watch?v=l1wHyMR_SCA**
24	The Camel Carol	**youtube.com/watch?v=-YsPTxokft4**
25	As with gladness men of old	**youtube.com/watch?v=sp52sx2_GYs**